Bertelsmann

This book analyzes one of the largest media conglomerates worldwide, the Bertelsmann Corporation. Analyzing its history, its corporate divisions, and international business relations, the book focuses on the dominant role of Bertelsmann in international media – and media services – in Europe, the United States, Latin America, and China. Addressing a broad readership interested in issues of media ownership, journalism, and policy work, this book shows how issues of media ownership and corporate power are closely connected to issues of beyond media, namely politics, consulting, services, and financial transactions. The book also draws parallels to other major media conglomerates and their attempts to influence communication infrastructures and policies on national and international levels, helping readers to understand the broader structural relations and power mechanisms at play in the global media market.

The book will be of interest primarily to scholars in the fields of global media studies, international communication studies, and the critical political economy of media and communication.

Mandy Tröger is a Walter-Benjamin-Fellow of the German Research Foundation (DFG). Her publications include: *Monopolizing the Democratic Dream: The Struggle over a Free Press in East Germany 1989/1990*, *International Journal of Communication* (2021); *Digitaler Kapitalismus. Die Macht globaler Technologiekonzerne* [Digital Capitalism: The Power of Global Tech Companies] (2021); *Pressefrühling und Profit. Wie westdeutsche Verlage 1989/1990 den Osten eroberten* [On the Rise and Death of Newspapers: How West German Newspaper Publishers Conquered the East in 1989/1990] (2019).

Jörg Becker is a Professor of Political Science at Marburg University, Germany. His latest book publications include: *Elisabeth Noelle-Neumann zwischen NS-Ideologie und Konservatismus* [Elisabeth Noelle-Neumann between NS: Ideology and Conservatism] (2013); *Medien im Krieg – Krieg in den Medien* [Media in War – War in Media] (2016) and *Gustav Flohr: Noch ein Partisan! Ein Remscheider Kommunist, Klempner, Spanienkämpfer und Bürgermeister* [Gustav Flohr: Another Partisan! A Communist, Plumber, Fighter in Spain and Major from Remscheid] (2020).

Global Media Giants
Series editors: Benjamin J. Birkinbine, Rodrigo Gomez, and Janet Wasko

Since the second half of the 20th century, the significance of media corporate power has been increasing in different and complex ways around the world; the power of these companies in political, symbolic and economic terms has been a global issue and concern. In the 21st century, understanding media corporations is essential to understanding the political, economic and socio-cultural dimensions of our contemporary societies.

The **Global Media Giants** series continues the work that began in the series editors' book *Global Media Giants*, providing detailed examinations of the largest and most powerful media corporations in the world.

Grupo Clarín
From Argentine Newspaper to Convergent Media Conglomerate
Guillermo Mastrini, Martín Becerra, and Ana Bizberge

Vivendi
A Key Player in Global Entertainment and Media
Philippe Bouquillion

Alibaba
Infrastructuring Global China
Hong Shen

Bertelsmann
A Transnational Media Service Giant
Mandy Tröger and Jörg Becker

For more information about this series, please visit: https://www.routledge.com/Global-Media-Giants/book-series/GMG

Bertelsmann
A Transnational Media Service Giant

Mandy Tröger and Jörg Becker

NEW YORK AND LONDON

First published 2023
by Routledge
605 Third Avenue, New York, NY 10158

and by Routledge
4 Park Square, Milton Park, Abingdon, Oxon, OX14 4RN

Routledge is an imprint of the Taylor & Francis Group, an informa business

© 2023 Mandy Tröger and Jörg Becker

The right of Mandy Tröger and Jörg Becker to be identified as authors of this work has been asserted in accordance with sections 77 and 78 of the Copyright, Designs and Patents Act 1988.

All rights reserved. No part of this book may be reprinted or reproduced or utilised in any form or by any electronic, mechanical, or other means, now known or hereafter invented, including photocopying and recording, or in any information storage or retrieval system, without permission in writing from the publishers.

Trademark notice: Product or corporate names may be trademarks or registered trademarks, and are used only for identification and explanation without intent to infringe.

Library of Congress Cataloging-in-Publication Data
Names: Tröger, Mandy, author. | Becker, Jörg, 1946– author.
Title: Bertelsmann : a transnational media service giant / Mandy Tröger and Jörg Becker.
Description: New York : Routledge, 2023. |
Series: Global media giants | Includes bibliographical references and index.
Identifiers: LCCN 2022036777 (print) | LCCN 2022036778 (ebook)
Subjects: LCSH: C. Bertelsmann Verlag. | Publishers and publishing—Germany—History. | Mass media—Germany—History.
Classification: LCC Z315.B53 T76 2022 (print) | LCC Z315.B53 (ebook) | DDC 070.5/0943—dc23/eng/20220902
LC record available at https://lccn.loc.gov/2022036777
LC ebook record available at https://lccn.loc.gov/2022036778

ISBN: 978-1-032-06896-1 (hbk)
ISBN: 978-1-032-10500-0 (pbk)
ISBN: 978-1-003-21560-8 (ebk)

DOI: 10.4324/9781003215608

Typeset in Times New Roman
by codeMantra

Contents

Acknowledgments vii

Introduction 1

1 **History and Family Ownership** 6
   1.1 Bertelsmann during the Nazi Era 7
      1.1.1 High Sales and High Profits 9
   1.2 Bertelsmann after 1945 11

2 **Bertelsmann Divisions and Corporate Strategies** 15
   2.1 Television, Radio, and Streaming: The RTL Group 18
      2.1.1 "Streaming Wars" 20
   2.2 Books and Magazines: Penguin Random House and Gruner + Jahr 23
      2.2.1 Penguin Random House 24
      2.2.2 Producing Bestsellers on End 25
      2.2.3 Gruner + Jahr 26
   2.3 BMG Rights Management 29
      2.3.1 A History of Alliances 30
   2.4 Arvato: Services and Finances 33
      2.4.1 History 34
      2.4.2 Divisions 35
      2.4.3 Solution Groups 36

3 **The Global Media Giant** 39
   3.1 United States: A Top Market 40
      3.1.1 Regulatory Framework and Revolving Door Practices 41
      3.1.2 Consumer Issues and Labor/Trade Union Responses 42

3.2 China: A Competitive Market in an International Context 49
   3.2.1 Successful Competitors and New Strategies of Bertelsmann 54
3.3 Latin America: "Export through Agents and Installation of Commercial Subsidiaries" 60
   3.3.1 A Media Service Giant in Latin America 65
3.4 Non-Places 68
   3.4.1 Tax Havens in Europe and Arvato in Ireland 71

4 The Bertelsmann Foundation: "Making Politics"   75
4.1 Influencing Public Debates 78
   4.1.1 "Privatizing Politics" 79
4.2 Revolving Door Practices in Europe 85
4.3 The Transatlantic Trade and Investment Partnership (TTIP) 87

5 Corporate Strategies   91

Concluding Remarks: A Transnational Information and Service Giant   96

Index   103

Acknowledgments

Over the years, Jörg Becker has written extensively about the Bertelsmann Corporation while Mandy Tröger's research has focused on broader implications of global capitalism on the transformation of media and communication and vice versa. This book has provided us with the opportunity to join forces. It contains an updated critical analysis of Germany's largest media service corporation, the Bertelsmann Group, and makes accessible German-language research for a broader English-language readership. We would like to thank Benjamin Birkinbine, Rodrigo Gómez García, and Janet Wasko for the opportunity to publish this book as part of their *Media Giant Series*. At Routledge Publisher, we are grateful for the help, support, and patience of our editor Emma Sherriff. Further, this book would not have come to fruition without the help of several people. We would like to thank (in alphabetical order): Laura Diaz (Universidad Nacional de Quilmes, Argentina), Daniela Inés Monje (Universidad Nacional de Córdoba, Argentina), Jingying Pan (Shanghai International Studies University, China), Rajeev Nathan Ravisankar (University of Oregon, United States), Kaifan Xie (Tsinghua University, Beijing, China). Last but not least, we would like to thank Pauline Köbele (University of Leipzig, Germany) for her excellent support in research and editing.

Introduction

To the general public, the name Bertelsmann stands for big business and philanthropy, namely for the Bertelsmann Group and the *Bertelsmann Stiftung*, the shareholding foundation of Bertelsmann Group. To researchers, however, the group and its foundation stand for a complex network of people and institutions, global market strategies, and overlapping political interests. Bertelsmann is one of the most influential media (service) giants in the world. Yet, headquartered in the small town of Gütersloh, Germany, relatively little is known about its activities. This is not a coincidence. The German magazine *Der Spiegel* once wrote that Bertelsmann, being "Europe's most powerful media company, is so big that it prefers to make itself very small [...] If there were an award for the world's most inconspicuous corporate headquarters, Bertelsmann would win it hands down" (Göttert, 2001, p. 15).[1] The divisions of the Bertelsmann Group include book and music clubs, music companies, publishing houses, television and radio stations, TV production companies, printing houses, as well as a range of (digital) media, industrial, and administrative service providers. Together, the Bertelsmann Group and its foundation can be thought of as global agents in the information industry. They are central players in knowledge and information transfer, in media production, and entertainment (Schuler, 2010). This book contextualizes the activities of the Bertelsmann Group, or the Bertelsmann SE and Co. KgaA, and the foundation in the contemporary global media economy.

Thomas Middelhoff, the former CEO of the Bertelsmann Group, once claimed that Bertelsmann "really [was] the most global media

---

1 Original: "Europas mächtigstes Medienunternehmen ist so groß, dass es sich am liebsten ganz klein macht .... Wenn es einen Preis für die unscheinbarste Konzernzentrale der Welt gäbe, Bertelsmann würde ihn mühelos gewinnen."

DOI: 10.4324/9781003215608-1

company" (Kirkpatrick, 2000) aiming to position itself at "the center of tomorrow's information society" (Drozdiak, 1998). Indeed, the Bertelsmann Group is Germany's largest media corporation and the largest media company in Europe. As a "media superpower" (Göttert, 2001, p. 15) it is also one of the largest media groups in the world. This makes the Bertelsmann Group Germany's only media conglomerate of "global significance" (Kleinsteuber and Thomaß, 2004, p. 133). In 2005, the group and its subsidiaries employed around 88,000 people in 63 countries, holding interests in more than 260 companies. That same year, the group recorded total revenues of around 18 billion euros, 30 percent of which were generated in Germany (Bauer, 2007). Fifteen years later, in 2020, Bertelsmann had increased its number of employees to 132,842 worldwide, with annual revenues of 17.3 billion euros (Bertelsmann, 2020). While these numbers come nowhere close to the big GAFAM players – namely *Google (Alphabet), Amazon, Facebook (Meta), Apple*, and *Microsoft* – the Bertelsmann Group invests heavily in digital services and infrastructures. It hopes to significantly increase its market share through further concentration (Krämer, 2021, p. 40). Bertelsmann's geographic core markets are Western Europe – in particular, Germany, France, and the United Kingdom (UK) – and the United States. In addition, Bertelsmann invests in growth markets such as Brazil and China. This book gives an overview of these markets, introduces the main issues, and underlines that market power does not lie in the market alone; it becomes manifest in policy work (Bertelsmann, 2010).

Today, the Bertelsmann Group is a sixth-generation family business run by the Mohn family. After World War II, the company rose from being a medium-sized enterprise to a major conglomerate under the leadership of Reinhard Mohn who, by favorable authors, is sometimes being compared to Bill Gates (Göttert, 2001, p. 12). While a family-run global conglomerate might seem strangely old-fashioned in a global communication economy that relies on transnational financial investments, still there are many family businesses in the media sector worldwide. This includes, for instance, the media empire of Rupert Murdoch (*Fox, News Corp*), the once huge publishing group of Robert Maxwell (*Daily News, Pergamon Press*), and the newspaper empire of K. K. Birla in India (*Hindustan Times*). or the TV group of Jeffry Koo from Taiwan (*United Communications Group*). Similar to media mogul Rupert Murdoch, who entered into a relationship with one of his interns,

Reinhard Mohn started a relationship with a telephone operator of his company. Elisabeth Beckmann, the telephone operator, became Liz Mohn. She is the current matriarch of the Bertelsmann Group, and one of the most powerful and politically most influential businesswomen in Europe.

The Mohn family currently holds 19.1 percent of the shares of the Bertelsmann Group, and Liz Mohn and her son Christoph Mohn are on the group's executive board (next to Thomas Raabe who has been appointed to the board in 2006, and who has been its chairman and CEO since 2012). The family's grip on the company is strong: In 2002, Thomas Middelhoff, then CEO of the group, wanted to list the company on the stock market. The Mohn family, wanting to save the family business model, short-handedly dismissed Middelhoff with a severance payment in the double-digit millions. Shortly after, between 2005 and 2006, the Bertelsmann Group took up an additional 4.5 billion euros loan. Why? The Mohn family wanted to buy back 25.1 percent holdings of the Belgian *Groupe Bruxelles Lambert* (GPB) to secure its future control over the group (Ferschli, Grabner, and Theine, 2019, p. 19). Until this day, the Bertelsmann Group is not listed on the stock market.

The majority of capital shares, namely 77.6 percent of the Bertelsmann Group, belong to the *Bertelsmann Stiftung*, a foundation founded by Reinhard Mohn in 1977. Mohn (long-term chairman of the foundation) initiated this transfer in 1993. In doing so, he not only secured the long-term control of the family over the company, but he also saved about 2 billion euros in taxes (see Chapter 4). Today, the Bertelsmann Foundation, according to the German business newspaper *Handelsblatt*, is "probably the largest, but definitely the most influential foundation in Germany," if not Europe (Frech, 2000). Financed by the profits of the company, in 2019, the foundation spent a total of 90 million euros for non-profit work (in education, healthcare, digital technology, etc.) closely related to company interests (Schuler, 2010). Among the foundation's four executive board members are Liz Mohn and her daughter Brigitte Mohn (Bertelsmann Foundation Annual Report 2019, 2020). Also the other 3.3 percent of the Bertelsmann Group's shares belong to foundations, namely the *Reinhard Mohn Stiftung* and the *BVG Stiftung*. Members of the Mohn family serve on the executive boards of both.

Though this book focuses on the traditional corporate group divisions (namely television and radio, books and magazines, music, and services), it also shows that the Bertelsmann Group has been trying to establish itself in online markets as early as the mid-2000s. With traditional media businesses, that is, the production and distribution of media content, becoming less and less important, the group has been expanding its business and corporate strategies. Bertelsmann holds stakes in all kinds of non-traditional marketplaces, startups, and media platforms (Hautsch, 2021a, 2021b). For instance, Bertelsmann and *Microsoft* are expanding their partnership, especially in the areas of cloud computing, artificial intelligence, and platform development. Their first project "BeData" – a platform for the analysis and use of consumer data – is already being used on the streaming portal *RTL+* (Gieselmann, 2021). In engaging with these new markets, however, Bertelsmann builds on monopoly structures, which it created in various traditional media markets for decades.

This book, thus, looks at the history, the corporate divisions, and international business relations of the Bertelsmann Group. It focuses on the dominant role of Bertelsmann in international media beyond the United States and European context. A particular focus is put on the United States, Latin America, and China. Addressing a broad readership interested in issues of media ownership, journalism, and policy work, this book shows how media ownership and corporate power are closely connected to issues of politics, consulting, services, and financial transactions.

References

Bauer, R. (2007, August). Global Player Bertelsmann. *Blätter für deutsche und internationale Politik*. Retrieved from https://www.blaetter.de/ausgabe/2007/august/global-player-bertelsmann [November 20, 2021].

Bertelsmann. (2010). *175 Years of Bertelsmann—The Legacy for Our Future*. Munich: Bertelsmann Verlag, Bertelsmann S. E. and Co. KGaA.

Bertelsmann. (2020). Bertelsmann facts and figures. Retrieved from https://www.bertelsmann.com/meta/facts-and-figures/ [August 30, 2021].

Bertelsmann Foundation Annual Report 2019. (2020). Retrieved from https://www.bertelsmann-stiftung.de/de/publikationen/publikation/did/bertelsmann-stiftung-annual-report-2019-en [August 12, 2021].

Drozdiak, W. (1998, May 13). Germany's media empire. *Washington Post*. Retrieved from https://www.washingtonpost.com/archive/politics/1998/05/13/germanys-media-empire/c0acb7e2-4785-4edb-b268-788e058cabbe/ [September 14, 2021].

Ferschli, B., Grabner, D., and Theine, H. (2019). *Zur Politischen Ökonomie der Medien in Deutschland. Eine Analyse der Konzentrationstendenzen und Besitzverhältnisse* (ISW-Report No. 118). Munich: Institut für sozialökologische Wirtschaftsforschung.

Frech, G. (2000, March 1). Die Zauberfrauen der sozialen Marktwirtschaft. Die Bertelsmann-Stiftung. *M-Magazin Verdi*. Retrieved from https://mmm.verdi.de/medienwirtschaft/die-zauberfrauen-der-sozialen-marktwirtschaft-29731 [July 10, 2021].

Gieselmann, T. (2021, November 10). turi2 am Abend: Google, Stefanie Kuhnhen, Zeit Online. *Turi2*. Retrieved from https://www.turi2.de/heute/turi2-am-abend-10-11-2021/?newsletter=true [October 21, 2021].

Göttert, J.M. (2001). *Die Bertelsmann Methode: Die 10 Erfolgsgeheimnisse des vielseitigsten Medienunternehmens der Welt*. Redline.

Hautsch, G. (2021a, July 22). Champions aus Gütersloh. *Junge Welt*. Retrieved from https://www.jungewelt.de/loginFailed.php?ref=/artikel/406844.globale-medienriesen-champions-aus-gütersloh.html [December 2, 2021].

Hautsch, G. (2021b). Gedrucktes unter Druck. *Marxistische Blätter*, Vol. 6 (2021), 28–38.

Kirkpatrick, D.D. (2000, September 3). Private sector; Not quite all-American, Bertelsmann is big in U.S. *The New York Times*. Retrieved from https://www.nytimes.com/2000/09/03/business/private-sector-not-quite-all-american-bertelsmann-is-big-on-us.html [December 5, 2021].

Kleinsteuber, H.J., and Thomaß, B. (2004). Medienökonomie, Medienkonzerne und Konzentrationskontrolle. In Altmeppen, K.D., and Karmasin, M. (Eds.), *Medienökonomie. Vol 2: Problemfelder der Medienökonomie* (pp. 123–158). Wiesbaden: VS Verlag für Sozialwissenschaften.

Krämer, H. (2021). Die Macht globaler Medienplattformen im »Online-Kapitalismus«. *Marxistische Blätter*, Vol. 6 (2021), 39–50.

Schuler, T. (2010). *Bertelsmannrepublik Deutschland: Eine Stiftung macht Politik*. Frankfurt am Main: Campus Verlag.

1 History and Family Ownership

Like most German media companies, Bertelsmann is also a family-controlled business: After World War II and under the leadership of Reinhard Mohn it rose from being a medium-sized enterprise to a major conglomerate. The Mohn family still holds 19.1 percent of the company's shares and Mohn's widow Elisabeth Mohn and his son Christoph Mohn are on the group's executive board. This chapter sketches the 185-year-long history of the Bertelsmann Corporation while focusing on the role of Bertelsmann in the Nazi era and the time thereafter.

The Bertelsmann Publishing House was founded in 1835 in the small town of Gütersloh (located in the Prussian province of Westphalia) by the bookbinder and printer Carl Bertelsmann. Westphalia, with its many liberal political clubs, played an active role in shaping the German Revolution of 1848/1849. However, the population of Eastern Westphalia, with its towns of Minden, Ravensberg, and Gütersloh, remained entrenched in conservative Protestant Pietism. It was this conservative Christian setting of a petty bourgeoisie that influenced the early business of the new book publisher. Book titles of the early years of Bertelsmann were related to the home, to church, or it were songbooks, such as *Die kleine Missionsharfe* (1853). This songbook was published in its 86th edition in 1941. By then, it had reached a total circulation of 2 million copies. Even more influential than the books published by Bertelsmann were its magazines and newspapers. For instance, with its *Volksblatt*, the Bertelsmann Publishing House placed itself at the forefront of the political counter-revolution in 1848. Also its conservative *Evangelisches Monatsblatt für Westfalen* soon had a circulation of 20,000 copies. It appeared until 1929 (Friedländer et al., 2002a, p. 23).

Bertelsmann produced popular and populist content aimed at Protestants who opposed modernization. While this was important for the publisher's self-image, the key to its success lay (and lies) in its distribution infrastructures. Bertelsmann's early Christian books were not aimed at individual readers in bookstores. They were sold to Christian associations, discussion groups, churches, confirmation groups, missionary festivals, poorhouses, schools, teaching institutions, and to the private high school founded by Carl Bertelsmann (p. 24). This means Bertelsmann focused on mass markets and efficient mass distribution of its products early on.

Bertelsmann's blend of Germanism and evangelical Christianity shaped the publishing house for more than 100 years. With the death of the publisher Heinrich Bertelsmann in 1887, the Bertelsmann family line died out. Heinrich had left no sons, only a daughter, Friederike Bertelsmann. She married Johannes Mohn, the son of a pastor, who then took over the Bertelsmann Publishing House. Until this day, his family name remains closely tied to Bertelsmann. In mid-2021, Bertelsmann spokesperson Liz Mohn passed her post to her son Christoph Mohn. Since the Bertelsmann Group is a sixth-generation Mohn family business (Jakobs, 2021).

1.1 Bertelsmann during the Nazi Era

On July 10, 1998, Thomas Middelhoff, then CEO of Bertelsmann, received the prestigious Vernon A. Walters Award from the *Atlantic Bridge* and the *Armonk Institute of the American Jewish Committee* in New York. In his acceptance speech, he stated:

> I consider myself fortunate to work for a company that has always supported religious and racial freedom. During World War II, we published books that were banned by the Third Reich as "subversive." Bertelsmann's continued existence was a threat to the Nazis in their attempt to bring freedom of expression under their control.
> (in Böckelmann and Fischler, 2004, p. 76)[1]

The point of Bertelsmann having been a threat to Nazi Germany had been so convincing that when Bertelsmann had bought out

---

1 Original: "Ich schätze mich glücklich für ein Unternehmen zu arbeiten, das sich schon immer für die Freiheit der Religionen und Rassen eingesetzt hat. Während des Zweiten Weltkriegs haben wir Bücher publiziert, die vom Dritten Reich als ‚subversiv' verboten wurden. Das Weiterbestehen von Bertelsmann war eine Bedrohung für die Nazis bei ihrem Versuch, die Meinungsfreiheit unter ihre Kontrolle zu bringen."

8 *History and Family Ownership*

the U.S. publishing group *Random House* just a few months earlier (which in turn had acquired the famous Jewish publishing house Schocken in 1987), the U.S. branch of the Jewish organization *B'nai B'rith* had welcomed the buyout in July 1998. It was even believed that the Bertelsmann Publishing House had been shut down by the Nazis. Bertelsmann's history, however, was not that glorious (Schuler, 2004, p. 137ff.).

In fact, the "resistance narrative" was eventually questioned publicly by German scholars (Böckelmann and Fischler, 2004, p. 71; *Jewish News of Southern California*, 1999). This resulted in rising public pressures on Bertelsmann in the United States, and the company felt compelled to establish an independent commission of historians to investigate its role during the Nazi era. The result of this investigation is the two volume publication *Bertelsmann im Dritten Reich* (Bertelsmann in the Third Reich). While containing valuable information about the complicated Nazi history of Bertelsmann, this commissioned work also downplays certain crucial political cruxes in this history (Friedländer et al., 2002a, 2002b).[2]

Under the chairmanship of Heinrich Mohn, the Bertelsmann Publishing House experienced an important phase of consolidation, modernization, and growth. This 30-year-phase began with Heinrich Mohn taking over the business in 1921 and ended with his son's, Reinhard Mohn, subsequent takeover in 1947. The years under Heinrich Mohn are intimately linked with National Socialism. Not surprisingly, one chapter of *Bertelsmann im Dritten Reich*, containing almost 40 pages, is exclusively dedicated to anti-semitic books published by Bertelsmann during that time. The authors of the study distinguish between four main anti-semitic topics: (1) The Jewish mission within Germany, (2) race and nationality, (3) theological discussions about who is "Aryan" and who is not, and (4) anti-semitic fiction (Friedländer et al., 2002a, p. 297ff.). Between 1932 and 1944, one of Bertelsmann's star authors was the Nazi poet and aggressive anti-semite Will Vesper. He had 13 book titles in large print runs, and Heinrich Mohn had made a personal effort to get him signed. Already in 1933, Bertelsman honored Vesper with a full-page advertisement featuring his portrait in a trade journal. That same year, on May 10, at the Nazi book burning (which Heinrich Mohn had welcomed

---

2 A theoretical classification of Bertelsmann's Nazi past reappraisal in comparison to reappraisal strategies of other companies with their "dark" stains is provided by other authors (e.g. Booth et al., 2007).

with a "hearty congratulations" [herzlichem Glückwunsch]), Vesper railed against Jewish influences on German society:

> We are at war [...] with an impudent, shameless, murderous society of rootless, all-poisoning and contaminating literati and Asiatics. And so nothing remains to be done but to struggle for the destruction of their or our spirit, for their or our kind in Germany.
> (p. 319f.)[3]

According to Bertelsmann's reappraisal of its own Nazi past, Heinrich Mohn was not a member of the Nazi Party NSDAP (but his sister Ursula, a commandant at the publishing house, was). Nevertheless, he was a member of several Nazi organizations, such as the *Reichsschrifttumskammer*, and other Nazi professional associations. Mohn also supported many Nazi associations and the NSDAP with financial donations; among other things, he was also a "supporting member" (Förderndes Mitglied) of the Schutzstaffel (SS), the black-uniformed elite corps and self-described "political soldiers" of the Nazi Party (Friedländer et al., 2002b). Ultimately, however, the question of the publisher's personal membership in Nazi organizations is less telling than his publishing policy.

1.1.1 High Sales and High Profits

Based on sales numbers, the Bertelsmann Publishing House was closely connected to the Nazi regime: The company generated its highest sales of more than 8 million Reichsmarks in the war year of 1941, and it had its highest number of employees in 1939 (440 employees) and in 1940 (436 employees) (p. 566). The most visible indication for the symbiotic relationship between the publishing house and the Nazi regime are the special book series of the Bertelsmann Publishing House for the German Wehrmacht. Of the many German publishing houses that supplied a total of some 18 million German soldiers and members of the Waffen-SS with entertainment and other reading material during wartime, Bertelsmann topped the list

---

3 Original version: "Wir stehen im Krieg [...] gegenüber einer frechen, schamlosen, mörderischen Gesellschaft wurzelloser, alles vergiftender und verseuchender Literaten und Asiaten. Und so bleibt uns gar nichts als Kampf bis zur Vernichtung ihres oder unseres Geistes, ihrer oder unserer Art in Deutschland."

with 19 million books only for this target group. Bertelsmann was ahead even of the *Eher-Verlag*, which belonged to the NSDAP. In spite of all free-market practices, for Bertelsmann this deal was a non-competitive, risk-free and, so to speak, sure-fire business. It was comparable to that of the German cigarette factory *Reemtsma* in Hamburg, which held the cigarette monopoly for the German Wehrmacht. The content of the Bertelsmann Wehrmacht books was less heavy on militarism and Nazi ideology but it focused on light entertainment: Although German classics as well as Nazi authors such as Will Vesper, Hans Grimm, and Kurt Ziesel were published, the bulk of books contained entertainment, suspense, and humor.

On May 1, 1933, the Nazis banned free German trade unions and replaced them with the German Labor Front (DAF). Under the ideological banner of German fascism, this association unified employers and employees within one community of interests, seemingly erasing their differences. This approach fell on fruitful grounds at Bertelsmann. The once Christian publishing house had always given great importance to a good working atmosphere: the management had always been concerned with the well-being of its employees, company celebrations and anniversaries had always been a welcomed occasion to celebrate the "Bertelsmann family." This is still the case. Also the profit-sharing model, which took different shapes after 1945, is still a defining feature of the Bertelsmann Group. This means Bertelsmann employees can purchase tax-saving shares (or benefit from the company's profits in other ways). The group pays out these shares as low-interest loans and, thus, receives a large inflow of capital. While this co-ownership model is available only for employees of the company, these employees (unlike traditional shareholders) are not entitled to vote on company matters (see Chapter 5).

After 1945, well-cushioned with financial reserves and 550 tons of paper from the Nazi era, the Bertelsmann Publishing House made a successful leap into a supposedly new era (p. 515). Of course, the publisher did not really have to make a new start. Bertelsmann's first book of fiction published after Germany's liberation was *Der Trost Gottes. Predigten in schweren Zeiten* (The comfort of God. Sermons in Hard Times) by Paul Althaus. This was in January 1946. It was an edition of 10,000 copies, a large print run for the time. At first glance, the title seems appropriate considering the disastrous postwar time in Germany. However, the story is more complicated than that. For decades, Althaus had been one of the most important theological authors of the Bertelsmann Publishing House. Within

History and Family Ownership 11

the Protestant church, however, he was also a notorious anti-semite. The first sermon in Althaus's 1946 book was from November 30, 1941 – a day when Hamburg was heavily bombed. It says: "In hard times, we should be hard on ourselves and brave. Jesus Christ is not a savior for sniveling people who want to escape internally from the outer harshness of our time" (Althaus, 1946, p. 13f.). Shortly before the end of the war, in April 1945, Althaus wrote that "the spirit and culture of our people were born and grew out of the encounter of Jesus Christ with the Germanic spirit" (p. 229).[4] As with Althaus, other fictional books from 1946 were little more than the exploitation of old Nazi stock.

"If you can't swim against the tide, then you'd better swim with it" – true to this motto, Heinrich Mohn, who had had an affinity for the Nazis, very quickly came to terms with U.S. occupation. Politically opportune, in 1946, he printed the new laws of the U.S. occupation government as well as new textbooks approved by the Allies. Their total circulation was 140,000 copies (Friedländer et al., 2002b, p. 497).

1.2 Bertelsmann after 1945

After 1945, Bertelsmann's market rise paralleled a more general economic boom in the Federal Republic of Germany (FRG), and Bertelsmann soon became one of the country's largest book publishers (Göttert, 2001, p. 17). In the 1960s, the company extended its activities to other European countries, in the 1970s it targeted the U.S. market (e.g. by acquiring 51 percent of *Bantam Books*). Bertelsmann increasingly faced anti-trust laws. For instance, in 1977, the Federal Cartel Office investigated Bertelsmann due to its planned purchase of the Munich-based Wilhelm Goldmann publishing house. Bertelsmann was already Germany's largest media group at the time, owning 80 companies and generating annual sales of 2.4 million Deutschmark in 1975/1976 with just under 22,000 employees. Though the Federal Cartel Office was concerned about the "financial resources" (finanziellen Ressourcen) of the group, it approved the merger after only a brief examination (see

---

4 Original version: "In harter Zeit sollen auch wir hart mit uns selbst und tapfer sein. Jesus Christus ist kein Heiland für wehleidige Leute, die sich der Härte unserer Zeit innerlich entziehen möchten" and "Geist und Kultur unseres Volkes aus der Begegnung Jesu Christi mit dem germanischen Wesen geboren und gewachsen sind."

Verflechtungen, Zusammenschlüsse und Verbindungen von Verlagen, 1977).[5] In the 1980s, when private broadcasting was introduced to the FRG, Bertelsmann invested heavily in commercial television, and by the 1990s, the company had become the world's second largest media conglomerate: It extended its business relations to Central and Eastern Europe, had about 350 direct subsidiaries and about 45,000 employees. In 1990/1991 alone, Bertelsmann reached sales of 14.5 billion Deutschmark, 63 percent involved business outside of Germany, mainly in the United States (see Becker, 2017, 1985a, 1985b; Böckelmann and Fischler, 2004; Becker and Bickel, 1992).

The Bertelsmann's book club model called *Lesering* (reading circle) was founded in 1950. It existed until 2014 and played a major role in the company's new upswing. At its peak in 1990/1991, the Bertelsmann *Lesering* had 7 million members. Gunter Ehni and Frank Weissbach (1967) found that just under half of all book club books were light novels (p. 86). Similarly, Michael Kollmannsberger (1995) found that the *Lesering* mainly promoted light entertainment literature and bestsellers (p. 132f.).

According to a 2017 study of the magazine *Lesering-Illustrierte*, which circulated in the book club, books were advertised to readers with slogans such as "treasures from father's bookshelf" (Schätze aus Vaters Bücherregal), "ornament to every bookshelf" (Zierde jedes Bücherregals) and "decoration of the home and at the same time a distinction for the owner" (Schmuck der Wohnung und zugleich eine Auszeichnung für den Besitzer). Many of the *Lesering* books were also bound in half leather and embossed in gold, which made them "valuable status symbols" (wertvolle Statussymbole) that "not only entertain or impart knowledge, but at the same time beautify the home, enrich our lives as good friends, and make ideal gifts" (Dumont, 2017, pp. 181–200).[6] In other words, Bertelsmann's books were accessories for those who climbed the social ladder during the German economic miracle of the 1950s and 1960s. Reading is related to one's social status, not to intrinsic

---

5 Never since its founding in 1958 has the Federal Cartel Office prohibited any of major mergers that led to increased concentration of the German media sector. Since 1977, German antitrust law has shifted away from the national and towards the European level. Currently, EU competition authorities supports large European media groups for them to compete globally.

6 Original version: "die nicht nur unterhalten oder Wissen vermitteln, sondern gleichzeitig das Zuhause verschönern, unser Leben als gute Freunde bereichern und ideale Geschenke sind."

motifs. The growth in subscribers to the Bertelsmann *Lesering*, therefore, stands for a more general depoliticization of large segments of the population, not for their increased politicization.[7]

References

Althaus, P. (1946). *Der Trost Gottes. Predigten in schwerer Zeit*. Gütersloh: Bertelsmann.

Becker, J. (1985a). Activities in foreign countries and new technologies of a transnational corporation: the example of Bertelsmann. *Media, Culture and Society*, Vol. 7 (3), 313–330. doi: 10.1177/016344385007003004

Becker, J. (1985b). Ein multinationaler Informationskonzern angesichts neuer Technologien: Bertelsmann. In: P. H. Mettler (Ed.), *Wohin expandieren Multinationale Konzerne?* (pp. 24–41). Frankfurt: Haag and Herchen Verlag.

Becker, J. (2017). Bertelsmann SE and Co. In B. Birkinbine, R. Gomez, and J. Wasko (Eds.), *Global Media Giants* (pp. 144–162). New York: Routledge.

Becker, J., and Bickel, S. (1992). *Datenbanken und Macht. Konfliktfelder und Handlungsräume*. Opladen: Westdeutscher Verlag, p. 107 ff.

Böckelmann, F., and Fischler, H. (2004). *Bertelsmann: Hinter der Fassade des Medienimperiums*. Frankfurt: Eichborn.

Booth, C., Clark, P., Delahaye, A., and Procter, S. (2007). Accounting for the dark side of corporate history: organizational culture perspectives and the Bertelsmann case. *Critical Perspective on Accounting*, Vol. 18 (6), 625–644. doi: 10.1016/j.cpa.2007.03.012

Dumont, V. (2017). Charakteristika der Literatur- und Buchdiskurse in den Mitgliederzeitschriften der Büchergilde Gutenberg und des Bertelsmann-Leserings in den 1950er Jahren. *Gutenberg-Jahrbuch*. Wiesbaden: Harrassowitz.

---

7 Many studies of the Bertelsmann *Lesering* confuse market enlargement with processes of democratization. These studies, commissioned by Bertelsmann, were put into place by (social democratic) scholars such as Wolfgang Langenbucher and Peter Glotz in the 1970s and 1980s. The reference to social democrats is important here because, for about 20 years, Bertelsmann had sought political proximity to this party. Communication researcher Peter Glotz was a managing director of the Social Democratic Party (SPD) from 1981 to 1987, and the former SPD federal finance minister Manfred Lahnstein worked on Bertelsmann executive and supervisory boards from 1983 to 2004. With the personal friendship between Liz Mohn and former German Chancellor Angela Merkel from the Christian Democrat Union (CDU), the Bertelsmann Group has long since moved closer to the conservative CDU. The most important CDU politicians with connections to the Bertelsmann Group are Tim Arnold, Elmar Brok, Horst Teltschick and Klaus-Peter Siegloch.

Ehni, G., and Weissbach, F. (1967). *Buchgemeinschaften in Deutschland*. Hamburg: Verlag für Buchmarkt-Forschung.

Friedländer, S., Frei, N., Rendtorff, T., and Wittmann, R. (2002a). *Bertelsmann im Dritten Reich* (Vol. 1). München: Bertelsmann.

Friedländer, S., Frei, N., Rendtorff, T., and Wittmann, R. (2002b). *Bertelsmann 1921–1951. Gesamtverzeichnis* (Vol. 2). München: Bertelsmann.

Göttert, J.M. (2001). *Die Bertelsmann Methode: Die 10 Erfolgsgeheimnisse des vielseitigsten Medienunternehmens der Welt*. München: Redline.

Jakobs, H.-J. (2021, June 11). Wachwechsel in Gütersloh: Liz Mohn übergibt die Macht bei Bertelsmann an ihren Sohn. *Handelsblatt*. Retrieved from: https://www.handelsblatt.com/unternehmen/mittelstand/familienunternehmer/medienkonzern-wachwechsel-in-guetersloh-liz-mohn-uebergibt-die-macht-bei-bertelsmann-an-ihren-sohn/27278168.html [March 9, 2022]

Jewish News of Southern California (1999, January 15). New owner Random House under scrutiny for wartime past. Retrieved from https://www.jweekly.com/1999/01/15/new-owner-of-random-house-under-scrutiny-for-wartime-past

Kollmannsberger, M. (1995). *Buchgemeinschaften im deutschen Buchmarkt: Funktionen, Leistungen, Wechselwirkungen*. Wiesbaden: Harrassowitz.

Schuler, T. (2004). *Die Mohns: Vom Provinzbuchhändler zum Weltkonzern: Die Familie hinter Bertelsmann* (Vol. 61572). Frankfurt/New York: Campus Verlag/

Verflechtungen, Zusammenschlüsse und Verbindungen von Verlagen. Zusammenschluss von Goldmann- und Bertelsmann-Verlag (1977). German National Archive Koblenz. B_145_11958.

2 Bertelsmann Divisions and Corporate Strategies

As a decentralized organization, Bertelsmann is involved in an entire range of media and communication markets and services (Bertelsmann, 2010; Lehning, 2004; Böckelmann and Fischler, 2004). This chapter looks at the different divisions and interlocking strategies by focusing on four (media and communication) markets: television and radio, books and magazines, music, and services.

In 2004, the company owned about 100 newspapers and magazines, 100 book publishers, about 12 printing facilities, 24 television, and 17 radio stations. With changing media markets, however, also the group's investment strategies have changed. In 2020, Bertelsmann held interests in 67 television stations, 10 streaming services, 38 radio stations, global production companies and a digital video network, and more than 300 book publishers on six continents (Bertelsmann Annual Report 2020, 2021). This list is not exhausting all business activities of the group, however. Operating in around 50 countries, not even the group's Public Relations (PR) office always knows the exact numbers (Göttert, 2001, p. 15).

Since 2016, the conglomerate has been divided into eight (now seven) separate divisions. This includes the *RTL Group*, *BMG Rights Management* (BMG), the *Bertelsmann Education Group*, the *Bertelsmann Printing Group*, and *Bertelsmann Investments*. The Bertelsmann Group also owns the service company *Avarto* with more than 65,000 employees worldwide and, since 2020, it is the sole owner of the world's largest book publishing group (based on revenue), *Penguin Random House*. The latter controls a quarter of the world's book market. Bertelsmann also holds the majority share in the international publishing group *Gruner + Jahr* (G+J). In early 2022, *G+J* joined the *RTL Group*, leaving seven Bertelsmann divisions (Bertelsmann Annual Report 2020, 2021, p. 5). While each division is largely independent, "all divisions work together under

DOI: 10.4324/9781003215608-3

the Bertelsmann Group umbrella to take advantage of synergies where these exist" (Becker, 2017).

In 2021, Bertelsmann investments in intangible assets amounted to 166 million euros and were attributed primarily to the *RTL Group* (for investments in film rights) and to *BMG* (for the acquisition of music catalogs). Similar to 2020, the majority of investments in properties, plants, and equipment (a total of 140 million euros) went to the service company *Arvato* (Bertelsmann Interim Annual Report 2021, 2021, p. 13).

This chapter looks at the different divisions of the Bertelsmann Group and their interlocking strategies by focusing on four (media and communication) markets: television and radio, books and magazines, music, and services. Since the advent of the internet, Bertelsmann has focused on digital growth (Göttert, 2001, p. 196ff.). For example, already in early 2000, it purchased and later sold shares of the online service *America Online* (AOL). It was also involved in copyright litigation with the commercial online music service *Napster* in 2007 (Becker, 2007). Nowadays the Bertelsmann Group is a core player in growing digital markets overlapping with its more traditional media business units.

While this chapter does not list the *Bertelsmann Printing Group* (see Chapter 2.4), *Bertelsmann Investments* (see Chapter 5), and the *Bertelsmann Education Group* individually, it cannot be stressed enough that all Bertelsmann divisions are closely related, in particular in exploring new digital markets. For instance, for some time now, the *G+J*, the *Mediengruppe RTL Deutschland* (*RTL Group*) and *Penguin Random House* have been part of the Bertelsmann Content Alliance. Consisting also of the film production company *UFA, RTL Radio Germany,* and *BMG*, the alliance aims to take advantage of intra-corporate synergies. It produces media content and formats across different markets and aims to push Bertelsmann common interests. A first collective venture was the Audio Alliance. It produces podcasts and audio-on-demand programs and publishes new products exclusively on its own platform *Audio Now* (Bertelsmann Content Alliance, 2019). In 2020, the international scope of the Content Alliance was broadened with its launch in the UK. *Fremantle, Penguin Random House UK*, the international imprint *DK* and *BMG* launched a joint podcast production as part of the Bertelsmann Content Alliance UK (Bertelsmann Annual Report 2020, 2021, p. 7).

The Bertelsmann Group also has an increasing presence in the "digital entertainment and online education" market (Germano, 2018) while simultaneously investing hundreds of millions of euros

Bertelsmann Divisions and Corporate Strategies 17

into its service segment *Arvato*. This is no coincidence. There are plenty of overlaps between these growth markets: According to Bertelsmann, education is one of the biggest sectors in the global economy. Already in 2015, in the *Education@Bertelsmann report*, Bertelsmann CEO Thomas Rabe identified the global volume of the education market as over 5 trillion US dollars. Underlining the growing demand for education and its increasing digitization, Rabe pointed to "online training in healthcare and technology sectors; universities for medical and human sciences, and services for the education sector" as three segments of interest for the group with a target of 1 billion euros (Bertelsmann, 2015, p. 29). Bertelsmann, thus, focuses on e-learning and healthcare education (i.e. with training for medical professionals) and currently aims to expand this engagement by means of further acquisitions (Bertelsmann, n.d.-a). For instance, in 2015, Bertelsmann acquired a controlling stake in the Alliant International University. This gave the company access to university data for creating a global research and data-sharing network in health and human sciences. Alliant has over 3,700 students on ten campuses in California, Mexico City, Tokyo, and Hong Kong. Before Alliant, Bertelsmann purchased *Relias Learning*, the leading U.S. provider of online training in the healthcare sector, and *Udacity*, an e-learning provider with 3 million students from 100 countries (Smith, 2015). This network of inter-related business strands allows Bertelsmann to profit from its existing knowledge and infrastructures while promoting and selling its products. For this, Bertelsmann also collaborates with other major players in the digital (technology) market. Currently, for instance, the group is expanding its portfolio in partnership with *Microsoft*. Bertelsmann's online-learning provider *Relias* is building its platform on *Microsoft*'s Azure cloud technology while also other online-learning providers of Bertelsmann will profit from the partnership. Also, Bertelsmann and *Microsoft* are planning on developing a series of highly scalable platforms to deliver personalized content ranging from news to entertainment to education. The initial project "Be-Data," a platform for analyzing and using consumer data for the production of personalized content and advertising, is already being used by the streaming service *RTL+*. In the future, this service will offer personalized video/TV, music, podcasts, audiobooks, and e-magazines. Here, the technology set up with *Microsoft* is to track and manage customer loyalty, subscriptions, and advertising (Bertelsmann, 2021a). Further, there is the Bertelsmann Collaboration Platform (BCP). This collaboration between *Microsoft* and the Bertelsmann subsidiary *Arvato Systems* is a key internal project for the group. With more than 5,000 tech specialists working across the globe and in different Bertelsmann divisions, the goal of BCP is to implement the group's tech agenda to improve performances (Bertelsmann, 2021a).

2.1 Television, Radio, and Streaming: The *RTL Group*

Bertelsmann has been involved in what was to become the *RTL Group* since the 1990s. Initially one of many shareholding companies, over time and under the leadership of Thomas Middelhoff, Bertelsmann prevailed over other shareholders – such as *Pearson TV* (UK) and *Groupe Bruxelles Lambert* (GBL) (Belgium) – and eventually acquired the majority share in 2001. Since then, the *RTL Group* has been responsible for a large part of Bertelsmann's sales and profits.

The *RTL Group*, or what Jörg Becker (2017) calls "the Bertelsmann TV empire," grew out of the Luxembourg-based radio station *Radio Télévision Luxembourg* (RTL). Since its beginnings in 1984, when *RTL* entered the German private television market (with investments of 500 million Deutschmark), the group has grown into the largest private television and radio operator in Europe. In 2020, *RTL* held interests in 67 television channels and 30 radio stations in 10 countries. In addition, the group offers ten national streaming services, content production and other digital services (RTL Annual Report 2020, 2021). In 2019, its overall revenue amounted to 6,651 billion euros with an increase in profit by 10.1 percent to 864 million euros. Since 2019, Bertelsmann CEO Thomas Rabe is also the CEO of *RTL* (RTL Annual Report 2019, 2020).

In 2005, Bertelsmann held up to 90 percent of the shares of the *RTL Group*. Attempts in 2002 and 2007 to take over completely failed due to financial and legal issues. Since then, Bertelsmann has changed its strategies. In 2013, it sold parts of its shares in free float, reducing its ownership share from 92.3 percent to 75.1 percent. With its 1.4 billion euros profit, Bertelsmann financed its digital growth (*Handelsblatt*, 2013).

Key business areas of the *RTL Group* are the *Mediengruppe RTL Deutschland* (Germany), *Groupe M6* (France), *Fremantle* (UK), and the RTL channels in the Netherlands, Belgium, Luxemburg, Croatia, and Hungary, and *Antena 3* in Spain. The *Mediengruppe RTL Deutschland* is the Group's largest business unit, located in Cologne, Germany. Since 2013, the group has also operated in

Table 2.1 German-Language Free TV Channels, Pay TV Channels and Streaming Services

Germany	Austria	Switzerland
Free TV	*Free TV*	*Free TV*
RTL Television	RTL Austria	RTL CH
VOX	VOX Austria	VOX CH
ntv	ntv Austria	ntv CH
Super RTL	Super RTL Austria	Super RTL CH
RTLZWEI	RTLZWEI Austria	RTLZWEI CH
Nitro	Nitro Austria	Nitro CH
RTLup	RTLup Austria	
VOXup		
Pay TV		
RTL Crime		
RTL Passion		
RTL Living		
GEO Television		

Southeast Asia. With its channels *RTL CBS Entertainment* and *RTL CBS Extreme* it broadcasts, for instance, in Malaysia, Thailand, Singapore, and the Philippines (Table 2.1).

In 2020, the *RTL Group* generated most of its revenues in Germany (about 1.96 billion euros), France (about 1.2 billion euros), and in the United States (about 1 billion euros), followed by the Netherlands, the United Kingdom, and Belgium (p. 61). Due to the COVID-19 pandemic and a general decrease in the TV advertising market, however, the *RTL* revenue fell to about 6 billion euros. Revenues came primarily from advertising (43.8 percent television, 3.5 percent radio), content production (20 percent), digital activities (17.5 percent), and platform businesses (6.7 percent) (RTL Annual Report 2020, 2021, p. 2).

In 2021, however, revenues and profits of the *RTL Group* rose again "to a record high" of 6.64 billion euros with a record profit of 1.45 billion euros. This was not only due to a strong growth in TV advertising but also in streaming revenue from *RTLplus* and *Videoland* (Netherlands). It increased by 31.2 percent to 223 million euros and so did the revenue of *Fremantle*, the *RTL Group*'s global content producer. According to Thomas Rabe, CEO of *RTL Group*, the successful year 2021 was "driven by the recovery of the advertising markets" and the "particularly dynamic" growth of streaming and content production (epd, 2022). Thus, most profits for the group lie with its London-based *Fremantle* – one of the world's largest developers, producers, and distributors of fictional and non-fictional media content, the producer of soap operas and game shows (e.g. *American Gods, American Idol, America's Got Talent: The Champions*), and streaming services (e.g. 300 YouTube channels, etc.). According to the Bertelsmann website, in early 2022, *Fremantle* had an international network of production and distribution teams located in more than 25 countries. They produced 12,700 hours of programming per year and distributed more than 30,000 hours of content worldwide (Bertelsmann, n.d.-b).

Thanks to *Fremantle*, the *RTL Group* is one of the world's leading producers of television content. With the streaming services (including *RTL+, 6play, Salto,* and *Videoland*), the digital video company *We Are Era*, and *Fremantle*'s more than 460 YouTube channels, the *RTL Group* is also the leading European media company in online video. The group's streaming revenue, thus, increased from 141 million euros in 2019 to 170 million euros in 2020 (RTL Annual Report 2020, 2021, p. 3). According to Thomas Rabe, *Fremantle* is targeting total annual revenues of 3 billion euros by 2025. To achieve this goal and keep pace with growing demands, the *RTL Group* plans to invest in all geographic regions and in all three programming pillars, namely drama and film, entertainment, and documentaries (epd, 2022).

The *RTL Group* further owns the ad tech companies *Smartclip* and *Yospace*, as well as streaming tech company *Bedrock*; it is part of the Bertelsmann Group's *Content Alliance*, thus, it works with other Bertelsmann divisions and other outside partners; while the group's international marketer is *RTL AdConnect* (RTL Annual Report 2019, 2020; also Becker 2017).

2.1.1 "Streaming Wars"

Since February 2021, the *RTL Group* is revising its brand architecture to create a uniform brand presence for which a large part of the *RTL Group* is being relocated from Luxembourg to Cologne. This is one of many steps to help face the increasingly strong competition of streaming services such as *Netflix, Prime Video,* or *Disney+* (Lückerath, 2021; Bertelsmann, 2021b). With this, the *RTL Group* is not alone. Traditional media companies, particularly in the United States, have been spending billions of US dollars in the battle with global platforms such as *Netflix* and *Amazon*. "As part of these so-called 'streaming wars'," the RTL Annual Report 2019 states, "Disney, Apple, ATandT/WarnerMedia and Comcast/NBC

Universal have all launched – or plan to launch – new streaming services" (p. 8). In turn, the *RTL Group* focuses on building "national streaming champions" (e.g. *TV Now* and *Videoland*) in European countries where the group already owns leading TV channels. Thus, while *RTL* continues to grow in its core media businesses (radio and television, partly by means of alliances with other European media companies), it currently invests heavily in digital media, local streaming services, and the development of advertising technologies (RTL Annual Report 2019, 2020). For instance, the group plans on co-operating with the U.S. company, *Amobee* – one of the world's leading technology groups for advertising technologies for agencies, brand companies, and major TV broadcasters such as *Fox*, *ITV*, and *Univision*. *Amobee* focuses on targeted advertising tailored to each individual customer with the promise of higher revenues for broadcasters such as *RTL* (*Frankfurter Allgemeine Zeitung*, 2021).

The *RTL Group* aims at complementing global services such as *Netflix*, *Amazon Prime*, and *Disney+*. For this, it plans on increasing its streaming content expenditures from 85 million euros in 2019 to around 350 million euros in 2025 (RTL Annual Report 2019, 2020, p. 8). The overall goal is a higher (linear and nonlinear) reach of individual customers with targeted and personalized content and to monetize that reach more effectively by means of significant investments in content, marketing, and platform development. The underlying financial requisite, however, is cost reduction. This means consolidation. Not surprisingly, the *RTL Group* is currently undergoing "a wide-ranging review to reduce costs" and the sale of several non-core assets (p. 9).

These are also the driving patterns behind current transitions in the production of journalistic content at *RTL* –technology-driven journalism, individualized by ad-based algorithms. Simultaneously, both the Bertelsmann Group and the *RTL Group* underline their commitment to diversity and democracy. *RTL*'s goal, for instance, is to "reflect the diverse opinions of the societies [it] serves" (p. 11) because a "healthy, diverse and high-quality media landscape is the foundation of a democratic and connected society" (p. 14). It aims to do so in its workforce, content, and business relations. How limited the group's vision of "journalistic balance" is, however, can be seen in its understanding of diversity, for instance, in its own workforce. Aiming for an equal representation of women and men across all management positions, no reference is made to issues of race, class, sexual orientation, or ethnic background. The group broadens its definition balance by audience demands, stating that "we must reflect the audiences we entertain, and so we embrace workplace diversity in gender, ethnicity, disability and socio-economic status" (p. 16). The question remains: How can the *RTL Group* appeal to profitable mass markets across national boundaries while including cultural, ethnic, or gender diversity in journalistic content? When "journalistic balance" is based on an advertising market "across Europe as one region" (p. 16), the answer is simultaneously complex and simple. Diversity, by default, becomes bound to market logic, and minority groups can be included only if profitable.

References

Becker, J. (2007). Forschungspolitische Notizen zu meiner Bertelsmann-Forschung, unpublished. http://profjoergbecker.de/Dokumente/autobiotexte/2007%20Bertelsmannforschung.pdf [November 22, 2021].

Becker, J. (2017). Bertelsmann SE and Co. In Birkinbine, B., Gomez, R., and Wasko, J. (Eds.), *Global Media Giants* (pp. 144–162). New York: Routledge.

Bertelsmann. (n.d.-a). Strategy. Retrieved from https://www.bertelsmann.de/bereiche/rtl-group/#st-1 [January 30, 2022]. https://www.bertelsmann.com/company/strategy/

Bertelsmann. (n.d.-b). Bereiche RTL Group. Retrieved from https://www.bertelsmann.de/bereiche/rtl-group/#st-1 [January 20, 2022].

Bertelsmann. (2010). *175 Years of Bertelsmann—The Legacy for Our Future.* Bertelsmann, S. E. and Co. KGaA. Munich: Bertelsmann Verlag.

Bertelsmann. (2015). Seven stories about new businesses. *What's your story? Education@Bertelsmann,* Vol. 3. Retrieved from https://www.bertelsmann.com/media/news-und-media/downloads/education-bertelsmann-whats-your-story-engl.pdf [January 25, 2022].

Bertelsmann. (2021a, November 11). Bertelsmann und Microsoft intensivieren Partnerschaft. Retrieved from https://www.bertelsmann.de/news-und-media/nachrichten/bertelsmann-und-microsoft-intensivieren-partnerschaft.jsp [February 10, 2022].

Bertelsmann. (2021b, February 18). Neupositionierung der Marke RTL. Retrieved from https://www.bertelsmann.de/news-und-media/nachrichten/neupositionierung-der-marke-rtl.jsp [February 13, 2022].

Bertelsmann Annual Report 2020. (2021). Retrieved from https://www.bertelsmann.com/media/investor-relations/annual-reports/bertelsmann-annual-report-2020-finance-engl.pdf [January 20, 2022].

Bertelsmann Content Alliance. (2019, April 29). Bertelsmann Content Alliance founds Audio Alliance. Retrieved from https://www.bertelsmann.com/news-and-media/news/news-detailseite_71232.jsp?atn=and-abp= [December 5, 2021].

Bertelsmann Interim Annual Report 2021. (2021). Retrieved from https://www.bertelsmann.com/media/investor-relations/interim-reports/bertelsmann-interim-report-2021.pdf [January 20, 2022].

Böckelmann, F., and Fischler, H. (2004). *Bertelsmann: Hinter der Fassade des Medienimperiums.* Frankfurt am Main: Eichborn.
epd. (2022, March 17). RTL Group steigert Umsatz und Gewinn auf Rekordhoch. *epd medien.* no. 54a.
Frankfurter Allgemeine Zeitung. (2021, October 22). RTL auf dem Weg in die neue Welt der Fernsehwerbung. p. 23.
Germano, S. (2018, September 18). Bertelsmann to merge unit that moderates for Facebook with a competitor. *The Wall Street Journal.* Retrieved from https://www.wsj.com/articles/bertelsmann-to-merge-unit-that-moderates-for-facebook-with-a-co [November 20, 2021].
Göttert, J.M. (2001). *Die Bertelsmann Methode: Die 10 Erfolgsgeheimnisse des vielseitigsten Medienunternehmens der Welt.* München: Redline.
Handelsblatt. (2013, April 29). Verkauf von RTL-Aktien: Bertelsmann nimmt 1,4 Milliarden Euro ein. Retrieved from http://www.handelsblatt.com/finanzen/aktien/aktien-im-fokus/verkauf-von-rtl-aktien-bertelsmann-nimmt-1-4-milliarden-euro-ein/8140096.html [January 2, 2022].
Lehning, T. (2004) *Das Medienhaus: Geschichte und Gegenwart des Bertelsmann-Konzerns.* Wilhelm Fink Verlag.
Lückerath, T. (2021, February 16). Fokussierung auf die Kernmarke: Aus TVNow wird RTL+. *DWDL.de.* Retrieved from https://www.dwdl.de/nachrichten/81569/fokussierung_auf_die_kernmarke_aus_tvnow_wird_rtl/ [January 12, 2022].
RTL Annual Report 2020. (2021). Retrieved from https://www.rtlgroup.com/files/pdf3/rtlgroup_annualreport2020.pdf [January 5, 2022].
RTL Annual Report 2019. (2020). Retrieved from https://www.rtlgroup.com/files/pdf3/rtlgroup_annualreport2019.pdf [January 5, 2022].
Smith, B. (2015, March 6). Media group acquires Alliant International, plans global network. *The Pie News.* Retrieved from https://thepienews.com/news/media-group-acquires-alliant-international-plans-global-network/ [January 12, 2022].

2.2 Books and Magazines: *Penguin Random House* and *Gruner + Jahr*

Two other Bertelsmann divisions, namely the profitable book publisher *Penguin Random House* and the struggling magazines division *Gruner + Jahr* (G+J, show how the group deals with past, current, and future struggles in ever-changing media markets. Both divisions have taken different paths in recent years – one expanded to become a global monopoly player, the other merged into a different Bertelsmann unit. Both fates reflect on how the Bertelsmann Group searches for strategies to expand traditional media in non-traditional media markets. Its apparent solutions are: synergies and economy of scale.

2.2.1 Penguin Random House

Penguin Random House is the top player in the international book market. It controls about a quarter of the global book production and is responsible for about one-fifth of the group's revenues. The division is a conglomerate of publishers made up of more than 300 imprints across six continents. Its book brands include *Doubleday, Riverhead, Viking,* and *Alfred A. Knopf* (United States); *Ebury, Hamish Hamilton,* and *Jonathan Cape* (UK); *Plaza and Janés* and *Alfaguara* (Spain); *Sudamericana* (Argentina); and the international imprint *DK*. Penguin Random House employs more than 10,000 people in 23 countries and publishes about 15,000 new titles per year. It sells around 600 million print books, e-books, and audiobooks in 200 countries (Penguin Random House, 2021). In 2019, the company's revenue amounted to 3.6 billion euros (Bertelsmann Annual Report 2019, 2020).

Penguin Random House has had its world leading role in book publishing since July 2013, when *Random House* (Bertelsmann Group since 1998) and *Penguin Books* (*Pearson Media Group*) merged. For some time after, Bertelsmann held 53 percent of the shares, while Pearson held 47 percent (Greco, 2019; Becker, 2017). In 2017, Bertelsmann increased its majority stake. Three years later, the groups bought the final 25 percent from *Pearson* for 675 million US dollars (Bertelsmann Annual Report 2019, 2020; Bertelsmann, 2019). Since 2020, Bertelsmann has been the sole owner of *Penguin Random House*.

Penguin Random House grows both in the digital and the print market. According to Markus Dohle, CEO of *Penguin Random House*, the book publishing industry has grown during the COVID-19 pandemic. In early 2021 Dohle stated that the pandemic has led to greater consumer spending on books, which made "this [...] the best time in publishing" (Luxner, 2021). Subsequently, *Penguin Random House* continues acquiring other big players in the book publishing industry: Only in November 2020, it announced a 2.2 billion US dollars bid to purchase the New York-based U.S. publishing company *Simon & Schuster* from *Viacom-CBS*, surpassing the offer of Rupert Murdoch's *News Corp*. *Simon & Schuster* is the fifth-largest English-language book publisher in the world by revenues. This deal would give *Penguin Random House* control of nearly one-third of English-language book sales worldwide and 70 percent of the literary fiction market, which would make Bertelsmann the biggest book publisher in the United States (Wood, 2021).

According to Dohle, the planned acquisition would allow *Penguin Random House* to generate global reach for its global content. It was, thus, a new chapter in the company's history (Börsenblatt, 2021). To *Viacom-CBS* the deal would bring in new capital to boost its video streaming endeavors competing with platforms such as *Netflix*. As of November 2021, however, the U.S. Department of Justice under the Biden administration filed an anti-trust lawsuit to block this acquisition (see Chapter 3.1). In the court filing, the Department of Justice stated that the merger "would give Penguin Random House outsized influence over who and what is published, and how much authors are paid for their work," which would lead to "substantial harm to authors" (Wood, 2021). The Department of Justice also stated that contrary *Penguin Random House*'s public statements that its acquisition of *Simon & Schuster* would make the publisher "a counterweight to Amazon's alleged buying power," internal documents showed that *Penguin Random House* indeed hoped the merger would make it an "exceptional partner for Amazon" (U.S. Department of Justice, 2021). The U.S. book market would, thus, turn into a monopoly-driven enterprise with long-lasting consequences for any content provided to consumers across the nation.

2.2.2 Producing Bestsellers on End

According to André Schiffrin (2000), a U.S. publisher who left *Pantheon Books* in 1991 when it was being sold off to *Random House*, large book conglomerates such as Bertelsmann are capable only of "wild speculations with potential bestsellers" (p. 65). Creativity or more experimental formats running the risk of not appealing to mass markets fall through the cracks. The book publishing history of *Penguin Random House* speaks to Schiffrin's observation: the publishing house bid 65 million US dollars for two books, one by former U.S. President Barack Obama and the other one by former first lady Michelle Obama. This was the highest book advance in history. It came as part of an auction that included bids from *HarperCollins* and *Simon & Schuster* for worldwide publication rights. The expectation was that – given the popularity of the Obamas and the anticipation around their books – global sales for both would surpass the bid (Reuters, 2017; Shephard, 2017). These hopes were not disappointed. In 2018, on its first-day sales in North America, Michelle Obama's memoir *Becoming* sold 725,000 copies (*The Guardian*, 2020). *Becoming* became the highest selling book of 2018, with a total of 10 million copies sold. This boosted Bertelsmann's total revenue figures for the year and was hailed as a great business move. "The book's strong sales are a boon for [Thomas] Rabe's strategy to bet big on publishing" (Turner, 2017), the *Wall*

Street Journal wrote. Only in 2017, after the group had increased its shares in *Penguin Random House*, Bertelsmann CEO Thomas Rabe had laid out Bertelsmann's goal in the United States: pushing revenues by 30 percent by 2020. Thus, about half of the 4.3 billion US dollars spent in mergers and acquisitions since 2011 went to the United States (Turner, 2017). Subsequently, for the fiscal year 2020, the United States accounted for 24.8 percent of revenues, second only after Germany (see Chapter 3.1).

In November 2020, also Barack Obama's book *A Promised Land* made first-day sale records. In the United States and in Canada, it sold 890,000 copies. By the end of 2020, a total of 2.6 million copies of *A Promised Land* had been sold (Bertelsmann, 2021). In addition to Barack and Michelle Obama's memoirs, the *Publishers Weekly* bestseller list for 2020 included eight other *Penguin Random House* books. This included *Where the Crawdad Sings* by Delia Owens (*Putnam* imprint, 1.13 million copies); *How to Be An Antiracist* by Ibram X. Kendi (*One World* imprint, 697,000 copies); *Little Fires Everywhere* by Celeste Ng (*Penguin* imprint, 597,000 copies); *Greenlights* by Matthew McConaughey (*Crown* imprint, 565,000 copies), and *Caste* by Isabel Wilkerson (*Random House*, 543,000 copies) among others (Bertelsmann, 2021). This shows *Penguin Random House* is at the forefront of serving mass markets with high-profit margins. Projects appealing to smaller diverse communities, by default, are not part of this scheme.

2.2.3 *Gruner + Jahr*

For years, *G+J* has been one of the largest premium magazine publishers in Europe. In fact, until a few years ago, *G+J* was the largest European magazine publisher and among the four German publishers with the highest circulation rates. With regard to advertising and sales revenue, it was even number two in Germany (Hautsch, 2021, p. 32). In the 1990s, *G+J* was also a big player in the newspaper business (partly in the United States). At the turn of the century, however, the company sold several regional daily newspapers and refocused on the magazine market.

Founded in 1965, *G+J* started as a "publishing house of alternatives" (Göttert, 2001, p. 42) incorporating a variety of formats.[1] Similar to the *RTL Group* and *Random House*, it was slowly acquired by Bertelsmann whose influence grew steadily between 1969 and 1973.

---

1 Original: "Verlagshaus der Alternativen."

Bertelsmann Divisions and Corporate Strategies 27

Eventually Bertelsmann took over the majority share, and since 2014, has been its sole owner (Bertelsmann, 2010, p. 210ff.). *G+J*'s main associated companies outside Germany include the *Groupe Prisma Media* (France), *Brown Printing Company* (United States), and *BODA Publishing* (China) (Bertelsmann Annual Report 2019, 2020; Becker, 2017). Until recently, publishing more than 500 magazines and digital products, *G+J*'s activities in the magazine market focused primarily on Germany and France. Group sales, however, fell from 3 billion euros in 2001 to 2 billion in 2013 to 1.1 billion in 2020. In response, *G+J* withdrew from numerous foreign markets, discontinued magazines (such as the *Financial Times Deutschland* in 2012) and withdrew from other publishers (such as *Motor Presse Stuttgart* in 2019). Most recently, it sold off its French business. In August 2021, Bertelsmann announced that *G+J* would lose its status as an independent division and become a subsidiary of the *RTL Group* (Hautsch, 2021, p. 32). The two companies merged at the end of 2021. Shortly after, the Bertelsmann Group transferred its Hamburg-based *G+J*, including the magazines *Stern, Geo,* and *Brigitte,* to the *RTL Group* in Cologne, Germany. In January 2022, the merger was completed, henceforth *G+J* has been a brand of *RTL Deutschland*. On the evening of January 11, the day of the merger, a one-time 61-second image film was shown simultaneously at 8:14 p.m. on all television channels of *RTL Deutschland* announcing that *G+J* had been merged into *RTL* with immediate effect (Bartl, 2022).

By means of this merger, the Bertelsmann Group expects to make use of synergies and to generate an additional 100 million euros, a quarter of which is to be achieved by means of cost reduction (a considerable amount in human resource). In this way, the group intends to improve its position in fighting international competition, especially from the United States (Krämer, 2021, p. 40). Simultaneously, the high-quality journalism of *G+J* magazines is now in the realm of the mass tabloid *RTL TV*. In response, several experienced and highly respected *G+J* journalists, employees, and managers have left the Bertelsmann Group (*Süddeutsche Zeitung*, 2021).

To make matters worse, *G+J* closed its press database in January 2022 to save costs. This full-text database contained articles that had been uniformly keyworded since 1973, mostly from external sources. It was the oldest press database of its kind in Germany and Europe, and its sale was somewhat a political scandal in Germany. The archive landed with a private history company that sells individually created birthday greetings with original newspaper clippings (Peters, 2021). While this is nice for well-off customers, *G+J* journalists are now lacking an essential prerequisite for quality journalism.

References

Bartl, M. (2022, November 11). RTL Deutschland und G+J sind jetzt eins – 7.500 Quadratmeter großes Waldstück wird zum Symbol. *kressNews*. Retrieved from https://kress.de/news/detail/beitrag/148704-rtl-deutschland-und-g-j-sind-jetzt-eins-7500-quadratmeter-grosses-waldstueck-wird-zum-symbol.html [October 13, 2021].

Becker, J. (2017). Bertelsmann SE and Co. In Birkinbine, B., Gomez, R., and Wasko, J. (Eds.), *Global Media Giants* (pp. 144–162). New York: Routledge.

Bertelsmann. (2010). *175 Years of Bertelsmann – The Legacy for Our Future*. Bertelsmann, S. E. and Co. KGaA. Munich: C. Bertelsmann Verlag.

Bertelsmann. (2019, December 18). Bertelsmann acquires full ownership of Penguin Random House. Retrieved from https://www.bertelsmann.com/news-and-media/news/bertelsmann-acquires-full-ownership-of-penguin-random-house.jsp?atn=andabp= [October 1, 2021].

Bertelsmann. (2021, January 13). 'A Promised Land' was 2020's bestselling book in the U.S. Retrieved from https://www.bertelsmann.com/news-and-media/news/a-promised-land-was-2020-s-bestselling-book-in-the-u.s..jsp [October 1, 2021].

Bertelsmann Annual Report 2019. (2020). Retrieved from https://www.bertelsmann.com/media/investor-relations/annual-reports/annual-report-2019-financial-information-2.pdf [September 1, 2021].

Börsenblatt. (2021, April 2021). Bertelsmann setzt neue strategische Prioritäten. *Börsenblatt*. Retrieved from: https://www.boersenblatt.net/news/verlage-news/bertelsmann-setzt-neue-strategische-prioritaeten-175131 [January 5, 2022].

Göttert, J.M. (2001). *Die Bertelsmann Methode: Die 10 Erfolgsgeheimnisse des vielseitigsten Medienunternehmens der Welt*. Redline.

Greco, A.N. (2019). The strategy of publishing. In Phillips, A.P., & Bhaskar, M. (Eds.), *The Oxford Handbook on Publishing* (pp. 190–205). Oxford: Oxford University Press.

Hautsch, G. (2021). Gedrucktes unter Druck. *Marxistische Blätter*, Vol. 6 (2021), 28–38.

Krämer, H. (2021). Die Macht globaler Medienplattformen im »Online-Kapitalismus«. *Marxistische Blätter*, Vol. 6 (2021), 40.

Luxner, L. (2021, March 10). 'This is the best time in publishing ever,' says Markus Dohle. *New Atlanticist – Atlantic Council*. Retrieved from https://www.atlanticcouncil.org/blogs/new-atlanticist/this-is-the-best-time-in-publishing-ever-says-markus-dohle/ [January 10, 2022].

Penguin Random House. (2021). Imprints. Retrieved from https://www.penguinrandomhouse.com/imprints/ [January 10, 2022].

Peters, G. (2021). Ein fataler Fehler Kommentar zur Schließung der Gruner + Jahr Pressedatenbank. Retrieved from http://www.info7.de/Ein-fataler-Fehler_Kommentar_20210206.pdf [January 30, 2022].

Reuters. (2017, February 28). Penguin Random House lands book deal with Obamas. Retrieved from https://www.reuters.com/article/us-obama-books/penguin-random-house-lands-book-deal-with-obamas-idUSKBN16830P/ [January 5, 2022].

Schiffrin, A. (2000). *Verlage ohne Verleger. Über die Zukunft der Bücher.* Berlin: Wagenbach.

Shephard, A. (2017, February 28). Barack and Michelle Obama are about to get paid. *The New Republic.* Retrieved from https://newrepublic.com/article/141022/barack-michelle-obama-get-paid

Süddeutsche Zeitung (2021, August 10). Wie Feuer und Wasser. Retrieved from https://www.sueddeutsche.de/medien/reaktionen-auf-mega-zusammenschluss-wie-feuer-und-wasser-1.5377703 [February 21, 2022].

The Guardian (2020, November 18). Obama's A Promised Land sells almost 890,000 copies on first day. Retrieved from https://www.theguardian.com/us-news/2020/nov/18/barack-obama-book-presidential-memoir-a-promised-land [January 11, 2022].

Turner, Z. (2017, March 28). Bertelsmann's record book deal with Obamas underscores U.S. Push; Having signed Barack and Michelle Obama to a two-book deal, Bertelsmann is finding U.S. politics to be good business. *The Wall Street Journal.* Eastern Edition.

U.S. Department of Justice. (2021, November 2). Justice Department sues to block Penguin Random House's acquisition of rival publisher Simon & Schuster – complaint – PRH and SandS: Case 1:21-cv-02886. *United States District Court for the District of Columbia.* Retrieved from https://www.justice.gov/opa/press-release/file/1445916/download?utm_medium=emailandutm_source=govdelivery [January 20, 2022].

Wood, H. (2021, November 2). US Department of Justice sues to block Bertelsmann's S&S deal. *The Bookseller.* Retrieved from https://www.thebookseller.com/news/us-justice-department-sues-block-bertelsmanns-ss-deal-1286740 [January 20, 2022].

2.3 BMG Rights Management

BMG Rights Management (BMG) is an international music company with 20 offices in 12 core music markets. Founded in 2008 and wholly owned by the Bertelsmann Group, its headquarters are based in Berlin, Germany. *BMG* combines the activities of a music publisher and a record label and has numerous subsidiaries and shareholdings, for example, *BMG Rights Management* (Europe) GmbH. In addition to Germany, the company is present in Australia, Brazil, China, France, Italy, Spain, the UK, the Benelux countries, the United States, Canada, and Scandinavia (BMG, n.d.).

BMG represents more than 3 million songs and recordings, including the catalogs of *Alberts Music, Broken Bow Music Group,*

30 Bertelsmann Divisions and Corporate Strategies

Bug, Cherry Lane, Chrysalis, Mute, Primary Wave, Sanctuary, and *Trojan,* as well as thousands of major artists and songwriters (Bertelsmann Annual Report 2020, 2021 p. 5). Its portfolio includes, for example, rights to works by David Bowie, the Rolling Stones, Jason Aldean, Iggy Pop, and Lenny Kravitz. Just in October 2021, *BMG* acquired Tina Turner's entire collection, royalties and assets, as well as the rights to name, image, and likeness. This was the company's biggest artist-related acquisition (Millman, 2021). More recently, *BMG* has also added films, television, and books to its portfolio.

The business model of *BMG* is one of synergies: The company provides musicians with services typically offered by music publishers and record labels. By means of an integrated infrastructure operated under one roof and with the same technology, *BMG* aims at maximizing efficiency (e.g. by integrating all its international offices in one management structure matrix).

In the 2018 fiscal year, *BMG* generated 545 million euros in revenues: rights and licenses accounted for 91.1 percent and products and merchandise for 8.9 percent; almost half of its revenues (44.1 percent) were generated in the United States (Bertelsmann Annual Report 2018, 2019). In 2020, *BMG*'s overall revenue was 600 million euros (Bertelsmann Annual Report 2020, 2021, p. 13). In the first half of 2021, it registered a revenue increase by 5.2 percent to 296 million euros (the year before it was 282 million euros) (Bertelsmann Interim Annual Report 2021, 2021, p. 13), with over half of the revenues (187.6 million US-dollars) being registered in the United States (Ingham, 2021). *BMG* invests heavily in streaming services, which in 2020 grew at a double-digit rate. Accordingly, the share of revenues from digital businesses in *BMG*'s total revenues increased to 62 percent (Bertelsmann Interim Annual Report 2021, 2021 p. 13).

2.3.1 A History of Alliances

BMG is a re-launch effort of Bertelsmann: In 1979, Bertelsmann had acquired *Artista Record*; in 1985–1986, it had bought *RCA records*, and in 1987, Bertelsmann had merged these and other subsidiaries under the umbrella of *Bertelsmann Music Group* (BMG) (Thompson, 2009). Covering a wide variety of genres, such as folk and pop music, one focal point was classical music. In response to declining sales due to increasing file sharing, Bertelsmann agreed to merge *BMG* with *Sony* in 2003. The move came in the aftermath of an attempted venture with the *Time Warner* music division. *Sony BMG* had a 25 percent market share at the time (Bertelsmann, 2010, p. 172ff.; Landler, 2003).

Three years later, Bertelsmann sold its subsidiary *BMG Music Publishing* to *Vivendi* and eventually divested its stake in *Sony BMG* in 2008. In consequence, the company was renamed *Sony Music Entertainment*. Bertelsmann, in turn, started *BMG Rights Management* in October 2008. Initially, the new *BMG* was to focus on the European broadcasting market. After the global private equity firm *Kohlberg Krafvis Roberts and Co.* (KKR) became the majority shareholder of *BMG*, however, the company started to expand internationally. Its first foothold in the U.S. market was the purchase of *Cherry Lane Music Publishing* in 2009, followed by several international acquisitions in 2010, including *Evergreen Copyright Acquisitions* (BMG, 2010). By 2012, *BMG* had copyright control over 1 million songs. In 2015, it purchased *Rise Records* and *Minder Music* while also having two Top ten chart entries and the U.S. number one album with Janet Jackson's *Unbreakable* (BMG, 2021a).

Though Bertelsmann took over full ownership of *BMG* in 2013 when it acquired all shares from *KKR* (BMG, 2013), *KKR* is still involved in the company. *BMG* and *KKR* have up to 71 deals going with a combined value of 1.17 billion US-dollars (Ingham, 2021). Just in March 2021, *BMG* and *KKR* announced a new alliance for the acquisition of major music rights packages. It is a joint venture to "pursue recorded music, music publishing and other music rights acquisitions" sourcing individual transactions to acquire music catalogs (BMG, 2021b). This new alliance is one among many. *BMG* is also working with the global gaming platform *Roblox*, to open up gaming opportunities for artists and songwriters, and in 2017, it agreed to enter a long-term exclusive agreement with *Netflix*. *BMG* is to administer the music publishing rights of the streaming service outside of the United States. *BMG* also acquired the majority stake in *Undercover*, a concert promoter, which opened up the opportunity to get involved with live entertainment (BMG, 2021a). These are a few examples. They show that *BMG*, like the Bertelsmann Group, is busy building alliances with a wide array of media and music-related businesses.

At the same time, *BMG* (like Bertelsmann) pays great attention to receiving positive PR. In response to the Black Lives Matter movement and to allegations about racism in the music industry (i.e. Annenberg Inclusion Initiative, 2019, 2021), for instance, Bertelsmann has touted *BMG*'s efforts to respond to racism and discrimination. It pointed specifically to *BMG*'s practices in reviewing contracts for Black artists seeking to identify and rectify inequitable royalty payments (Bertelsmann, 2021a) (see also Chapter 3.1). Indeed, *BMG* carried out an assessment to identify inequity in its contractual terms with Black artists. The company's analysis found that "four of the 33 labels in the historically acquired catalogs have statistically significant differences between royalty rates for Black and non-Black artists" (Bertelsmann, 2021b). The company made clear, however, that it had not been involved in setting up the initial deals. It also underlined its intention to make changes benefiting recording artists (Bertelsmann, 2021b). A Bertelsmann press release even noted that the Black Music Action Coalition had highlighted *BMG*'s initiatives on reassessing contracts (Bertelsmann, 2021c). In spite of these efforts, however, it should be noted that these initiatives took place only *after* protests against the industry threatened the public image of *BMG* and other record labels, as well as their potential sales and future contracts. These initiatives are, thus, not intrinsically motivated but reactionary in essence. The overarching goal is to avoid financial losses.

References

Annenberg Inclusion Initiative. (2019). *Inclusion in the Recording Studio.* University of Southern California. Retrieved from https://assets.uscannenberg.org/docs/aii-inclusion-recording-studio2021.pdf [October 2, 2021].

Annenberg Inclusion Initiative. (2021). *Inclusion in the Music Business: Gender and Race/Ethnicity across Executives, Artists and Talent Teams.* University of Southern California. Retrieved from https://assets.uscannenberg.org/docs/aii-inclusion-music-industry-2021-06-14.pdf [October 2, 2021].

Bertelsmann. (2010). *175 Years of Bertelsmann—The Legacy for Our Future.* Munich: Bertelsmann Verlag, Bertelsmann S. E. and Co. KGaA.

Bertelsmann. (2021a). BMG and KKR join forces to acquire music rights. Retrieved from https://www.bertelsmann.com/news-and-media/news/bmg-and-kkr-join-forces-to-acquire-music-rights.jsp [September 20, 2021].

Bertelsmann. (2021b, January 4). BMG pledges action on historic royalties review. Retrieved from https://www.bertelsmann.com/corporate-responsibility/engagement/project/bmg-pledges-action-on-historic-royalties-review.jsp [September 23, 2021].

Bertelsmann. (2021c, July 8). BMG lauded for anti-racism commitment. *MarketScreener.* Retrieved from https://www.marketscreener.com/quote/stock/BERTELSMANN-SE-CO-KGAA-6500476/news/Bertelsmann-BMG-Lauded-For-Anti-Racism-Commitment-35819777/ [September 23, 2021].

Bertelsmann Annual Report 2018. (2019). Retrieved from https://www.bertelsmann.com/media/investor-relations/annual-reports/bertelsmann-annual-report-2018-finance-engl.pdf [January 20, 2022].

Bertelsmann Annual Report 2020. (2021). Retrieved from https://www.bertelsmann.com/media/investor-relations/annual-reports/bertelsmann-annual-report-2020-finance-engl.pdf [January 20, 2022].

Bertelsmann Interim Annual Report 2021. (2021). Retrieved from https://www.bertelsmann.com/media/investor-relations/interim-reports/bertelsmann-interim-report-2021.pdf [January 20, 2022].

BMG. (n.d.). About us. Retrieved from https://www.bmg.com/de/about.html [October 30, 2021].

BMG. (2010, September 28). US: BMG acquires Evergreen Copyrights. Retrieved from https://www.bmg.com/de/news/bmg-acquires-evergreen-copyrights.html [October 19, 2021].

BMG. (2013, March 1). Bertelsmann acquires full ownership of BMG. Retrieved from https://bmg.com/it/news/intl-bertelsmann-acquires-full-ownership-of-bmg.html [October 13, 2021].

BMG. (2021a). *About*. Retrieved from https://www.bmg.com/us/about.html [January 20, 2022].

BMG. (2021b, March 10). INTL: BMG and KKR join forces to acquire music rights. Retrieved from https://www.bmg.com/de/news/bmg-and-kkr-join-forces-to-acquire-music-rights.html [February 21, 2022].

Ingham, T. (2021, August 31). BMG revenues up 9% in first half of 2021... and it has over $1BN of acquisition deals in play with KKR. *Music Business Worldwide*. Retrieved from https://www.musicbusinessworldwide.com/bmg-revenues-up-9-in-first-half-of-2021-and-it-has-over-1bn-of-acquisition-deals-in-play-with-kkr/ [September 23, 2021].

Landler, M. (2003, November 7). 2 giants take steps to merge music units; Bertelsmann deal with Sony responds to plummeting sales. *The International Herald Tribune*.

Millman, E. (2021, October 5). Another blockbuster deal: Tina Turner sells entire catalog to BMG. *Rolling Stone*. Retrieved from https://www.rollingstone.com/pro/news/tina-turner-catalog-bmg-1236416/ [November 12, 2021].

Thompson, J.B. (2009). Trade publishing. In A.P. Phillips, and M. Bhaskar (Eds.), *The Oxford Handbook on Publishing* (pp. 245–258). Oxford University Press.

2.4 *Arvato*: Services and Finances

Arvato is a globally operating company offering a whole range of technical and administrative services to a wide variety of interested parties. It is wholly owned by Bertelsmann and a major division within the group. Together with the *Bertelsmann Printing Group*, which was founded in 2016, *Arvato* is the service segment of the Bertelsmann Group. In its current form *Arvato* was created in 1999. At the time, Bertelsmann's printing and industrial divisions were restructured, and more weight was given to services (Bertelsmann, 2010, p. 332).

Headquartered also in Gütersloh, Germany, *Arvato* has locations in at least 22 countries, including the People's Republic of China

(PRC) and the United States. In 2019, *Arvato* had about 77,300 employees. By 2021, this number had grown to 85,660 employees. While in 2019, *Arvato* generated 4.18 billion euros in revenue, by 2020, this number had grown to 4.4 billion euros (Bertelsmann Annual Report 2019, 2020; Bertelsmann Annual Report 2020, 2021). Currently, Bertelsmann generates about one-fifth of its revenue with the services offered by *Arvato*.

While *Arvato* operates service centers and IT systems for its customers (e.g. as a payment service provider), it also develops and implements logistics and financial services (e.g. services in credit checks, debt collection, customer relationship management (CRM), supply chain management (SCM), information technology, etc.). Focusing on "innovations in automation as well as data and analytics" (Bertelsmann, n.d.), *Arvato* provides services for global companies from telecommunication and energy providers to banks and insurance companies, to e-commerce, IT, and internet providers. Since January 2019, the Bertelsmann services business also includes the *Majorel Group*. Bertelsmann owns almost 40 percent of its shares (Bertelsmann, 2010, p. 332ff.).

2.4.1 History

Arvato roots in Bertelsmann's early logistics efforts: To meet demands from the *Lesering* (see Chapter 1) and the *Schallplattenring* (record ring), Bertelsmann massively expanded its warehouse and shipping capacities in the mid-1950s. In 1959, it founded the *Kommissionshaus Buch und Ton* (commission house book und sound) opening up its production and service infrastructures to other publishers. In the sole ownership of Reinhard Mohn, Bertelsmann benefited from this company because of economies of scale. The takeover of a punch card index from *Lufthansa* airline at the *Leesering* headquarters then laid the foundation for the company's IT expertise. In 1968, it eventually became the *Vereinigte Verlagsauslieferung* (VVA), based in Gütersloh, Germany. The purpose of this company was to deliver printing products and records for third parties (Bertelsmann, 2010, p. 342ff.; Arvato Bertelsmann, n.d.).

Bertelsmann took a similar approach with its printing plants, which had been bundled in the *Mohndruck* company since 1948. In the 1960s, after having purchased high-performance machines that required high-capacity use, the company focused on acquiring third-party orders. In the 1970s and 1980s, Bertelsmann founded and purchased additional printing and logistics service providers in France, the UK, Spain, and other European countries

(Bertelsmann, 2010, p. 340ff.). These became part of *Bertelsmann's Printing and Industry* division. From 1976, this division was headed by Mark Wössner, who later became Bertelsmann Chairman and CEO. Under his leadership, the service division of Bertelsmann expanded further. For instance, in 1983, it started distributing software and computers (p. 350ff.). By the mid-1980s, the Bertelsmann revenue share of its print and industrial division (including services) had reached more than 20 percent. In the late 1980s, the division expanded its involvement in the United States, and in the 1990s, it gained two important service customers: In 1993, it launched the *Miles and More* bonus program on behalf of *Lufthansa* while *Microsoft* (in the wake of the launch of Windows 95) transferred its customer services for Germany, Austria, and Switzerland to Bertelsmann (p. 361ff.). A joint venture with the German Postal Service *Deutsche Post AG* in 1994 gave Bertelsmann a lead position for address management solutions in Germany. It is worth mentioning that until this day, this joint venture, the *Deutsche Post Adress*, has a de facto monopoly on forwarding mail orders to relocation addresses in Germany.

In 1996, with Bertelsmann wanting to further expand its service sector, the *Printing and Industry* division merged under the umbrella of *Bertelsmann Industrie*. At this time, the company had around 12,600 employees worldwide and generated revenues of 3.28 billion Deutschmark. Only in 1999, the company was renamed *Bertelsmann Arvato*. The name (a neologism with no special meaning) was intended to reflect a change from a printing and industrial division to an international communications and media services provider. Soon, also *Sonopress's record* and CD pressing plants as well as encyclopedia publishers were incorporated in *Arvato Bertelsmann*. In 2002, the company eventually dropped the Bertelsmann-prefix from its corporate name (though it still uses it in its logo) (p. 364ff.).

2.4.2 Divisions

In its early years, *Arvato* was split into five divisions, namely into *Print* (printing), *Services* (distribution and logistics), *Storage Media* (storage media), and *Systems* (IT and data centers). Due to declining catalog and magazine circulations, *Arvato* also founded *Prinovis* – together with the German publishing house *Axel Springer* and the Bertelsmann subsidiary *G+J*. In 2005, *Prinovis* was the market leader in gravure printing in Europe (Bertelsmann, 2010, p. 339ff.). At the same time, *Arvato* started to offer public-sector services. Its first customer was the county of East Riding in Yorkshire, England. Under the banner of public–private partnerships, *Arvato*, from 2005 until 2013, took over public administration at the municipal level. This included, for instance, allocating housing subsidies, collecting local taxes or paying social benefits (Becker, 2017; Schuler 2010, p. 177ff.).

In the following years, distribution and logistics became more important. Therefore, in 2007, the business units dedicated to direct and logistics services were united under the umbrella of *Arvato Services*. It served companies in the IT and high-tech industries as well as internet and mobile communications companies. Since the Yorkshire public–private partnership, however, *Arvato* has also benefited from the outsourcing efforts in the public sector and has gained ground in serving public institutions and administrations (e.g. city councils, public offices, etc.). In Germany, *Arvato* is currently at the forefront of conservative think tanks promoting the privatization of public facilities and services (e.g. schools, roads, hospitals, cultural facilities, etc.) (Schuler, 2010, p. 176ff.).

At the turn of 2007/2008, Rolf Buch became *Arvato*'s new CEO, after the former CEO, Hartmut Ostrowski, was appointed CEO of Bertelsmann. While Ostrowski had pushed *Arvato*'s international expansion, Buch put more focus on three-dimensional growth, namely on new products, new customers, and on expanding the company's activities in its core markets (Bertelsmann, 2010, p. 366).

By the end of 2012, Buch was succeeded by former *Microsoft* manager Achim Berg who masterminded the acquisition of the insolvent e-commerce service provider *Netrada* in 2014. This led to a massive expansion of the company's position in integrated e-commerce services (Arvato Bertelsmann, 2014). Two years later, Berg left *Arvato*, which was then the *Arvato* Executive Board was completely dissolved (Wesseler, 2015). Since then, *Arvato* has been located and managed from within the Bertelsmann headquarters. In 2016, the company *Arvato AG* was merged into the parent company Bertelsmann SE and Co. KGaA, and it was deleted from the commercial register. The company is now run by a management board at Bertelsmann.

2.4.3 Solution Groups

Since 2014, *Arvato* has been organized in so-called Solution Groups. These groups are not structured according to products or technologies but according to customer requirements and businesses. Working independently, each group is headed by a managing director or chief executive officer. There are currently three Solution Groups, namely *Arvato Financial Solutions* (financial services), *Arvato Supply*

Chain Solutions (supply chain management), and *Arvato Systems* (IT services) as well as the *Majorel* group of companies (customer relationship management), in which Bertelsmann owns 40 percent of shares (Bertelsmann, 2021, p. 15 ff). With more than 48,000 employees in 28 countries in 2018, *Majorel* is a leading customer service provider in Europe, the Middle East, and Africa. It also has a strong presence in the Americas and Asia (Bertelsmann, 2019) (Table 2.2).

Table 2.2 Services of Arvato (2021)

Arvato Financial Solutions

Arvato Financial Services includes payment processing (e.g. invoicing, accounting, and payment) as well as factoring and debt collection (e.g. first- party or third- party collection). The division is active in consumer credit assessment, fraud prevention, and risk management. Arvato Financial Solutions employs about 7,000 IT, analytical, and legal experts in 15 countries. Its focus is on Europe. Services are provided for banks and credit unions, digital businesses, the healthcare and insurance sector, for media and entertainment companies, and the energy and mobility sector.

Arvato Supply Chain Solutions

Working in the technology, healthcare, telecommunication, automotive, banks and insurance, and publishing sector, Arvato Supply Chain Solutions offers a range of services around supply chain management (e.g. distribution, inventory, and quality management) and corporate information management (e.g. services relating to the logistics of marketing and sales materials). This includes logistics and fulfillment (e.g. warehousing, returns management), transport management (e.g. tracking, communication), order-to-cash management (e.g. invoicing, order management, customer service), technology (e.g. IT-architecture, robot controlled automation), and e-commerce (e.g. online platform development, loyalty management). This includes also after sales solutions: Arvato handles all services that arise after the sale of third-party products to end consumers, including the repair and reconditioning of defective devices (e.g. cell phones).

Arvato Systems

Arvato Systems focuses on digitizing corporate processes and business models by offering consultation, solutions, and products, as well as the operation and support of IT services. Target industries are the media, energy and utilities, and healthcare sectors as well as retail and consumer goods. The company is a multi-cloud provider. In addition to its own private cloud infrastructures, it offers so-called managed services for the use of public cloud providers such as Microsoft Azure, Google, and Amazon Web Services.

(Continued)

CRM Solutions and Customer Services (Majorel)

CRM Solutions and Customer Services offers classic customer communication, consulting services and digital solutions. For this, Arvato joined forces with the Moroccan Saham Group. In 2019, they founded the company Majorel. It is specialized in customer relationship management services (e.g. customer service from social media and online channels to automated interaction, artificial intelligence, analytics, self-services, and customer lifecycle solutions) and all related activities for private and public clients (e.g. call centers, data mining). Also approximately 600 employees, checking entries for Facebook for not complying with the network's community standards, are assigned to this unit.

References

Arvato Bertelsmann. (2014, February 7). Arvato kauft Netrada. Retrieved from https://arvato-supply-chain.com/media-center/presse-und-news/pressemitteilung/arvato-kauft-netrada [January 19, 2021].
Arvato Bertelsmann. (n.d). *About Us*. Retrieved from https://finance.arvato.com/en/about-us/corporate-history/ [January 19, 2021].
Becker, J. (2007). Forschungspolitische Notizen zu meiner Bertelsmann-Forschung, unpublished. http://profjoergbecker.de/Dokumente/autobiotexte/2007%20Bertelsmannforschung.pdf [November 22, 2021].
Becker, J. (2017). Bertelsmann SE and Co. In Birkinbine, B., Gomez, R., & Wasko, J. (Eds.), *Global Media Giants* (pp. 144–162). New York: Routledge.
Bertelsmann. (n.d.). *Arvato*. Retrieved from https://www.bertelsmann.com/divisions/arvato/#st-1 [January 29, 2022].
Bertelsmann. (2010). *175 Years of Bertelsmann—The Legacy for Our Future*. Bertelsmann S. E. and Co. KGaA. Munich: Bertelsmann Verlag.
Bertelsmann. (2019, February 19). *"Majorel" startet mit ambitionierter Wachstumsstrategie*. Retrieved from https://www.bertelsmann.de/news-und-media/nachrichten/majorel-startet-mit-ambitionierter-wachstums-strategie.jsp [September 13, 2021].
Bertelsmann Annual Report 2019. (2020). Retrieved from https://www.bertelsmann.com/media/investor-relations/annual-reports/annual-report-2019-financial-information-2.pdf [January 20, 2022].
Bertelsmann Annual Report 2020. (2021). Retrieved from https://www.bertelsmann.com/media/investor-relations/annual-reports/bertelsmann-annual-report-2020-finance-engl.pdf [January 20, 2022].
Schuler, T. (2010). *Bertelsmannrepublik Deutschland: Eine Stiftung macht Politik*. Frankfurt am Main: Campus Verlag.
Wesseler, B. (2015, July 10). Bertelsmann reorganisiert Arvato – wieder. *IT-Zoom*. Retrieved from https://www.it-zoom.de/dv-dialog/e/bertelsmann-reorganisiert-it-tochter-arvato-11054/ [December 5, 2021].

3 The Global Media Giant

The Bertelsmann Group is a global media (service) provider. This chapter looks at the group's business activities in the United States, Latin America, and China, while also taking a closer look at its subsidiaries in global tax havens. With the acquisition of the world's largest general interest publisher *Random House*, the Bertelsmann Group became one of the most important media players in the United States. At the latest since this entry into the domestic U.S. market, the Bertelsmann Group has influenced transatlantic relations, advocating, for instance, the Transatlantic Trade and Investment Partnership (TTIP). Since the 1960s, Bertelsmann – as a kind of expansion of its activities in fascist Spain – has also been exploring the Latin American market. Since then, Latin America has become a market of its own. With its diverse activities, the group concentrates on the three major (book) countries: Mexico, Brazil, and Argentina. Only recently did Bertelsmann discover China as a new wholesale market. But it has since entered it with all the more power. The group found its own ways to deal with many restrictive guidelines from the Chinese government. The Bertelsmann Group also has several subsidiaries in the Canary Islands and other global tax havens. This chapter looks at all of them.

The underlying question is, however, why does a company headquartered in Güthersloh, Germany start investing abroad in the first place? There are classic economic answers to this question: (1) Growth and an exhausted domestic German market. (2) Predatory competition from foreign competitors. (3) Investment opportunities under comparative cost advantages compared to Germany (lower labor protection, lower union organization, lower consumer protection, etc.). (4) Lower wages abroad. (5) The exploration of potential new markets for new products and services. (6) The takeover of foreign domestic publishers. Given the unequal power structures between industrialized countries in Europe or North America and

DOI: 10.4324/9781003215608-4

countries in the global south, investments in the latter make it possible for European or North American companies to generate extra profits. These classic economic conditions of global capitalism apply differently to Bertelsmann's activities around the world.

3.1 United States: A Top Market

Bertelsmann has been active in the United States since the 1960s. However, with the acquisition of the world's largest general interest publisher *Random House*, the Bertelsmann Group became one of the most important media players in the United States and worldwide. In 2020, the United States accounted for 24.8 percent of the group's revenues, second only after Germany (Bertelsmann Annual Report, 2020). Given the size of the U.S. domestic market and the central role of the United States in the global economy, Bertelsmann's initiatives to gain a foothold in it have been crucial in the company becoming a global conglomerate.[1] Its expansion in the United States coincided with a general shift in the U.S.–German relations and the onset of U.S. free trade policies and deregulation (Drozdiak, 1998). Bertelsmann's global ambitions were spurred in part also by increasing limits to further growth in Germany (Berghoff, 2013). Initially, however, the company's U.S. expansion under the leadership of Mark Wössner did not yield any significant profits. This changed only after 1998 with the purchase of *Random House* (see Chapter 2.2). By 2000, the United States accounted for 33.8 percent of Bertelsmann revenues (Reference for Business, 2021).

The purchase of *Bantam Books* in 1981 (after having taken over its majority share in 1977) marked the entry of Bertelsmann into the U.S. book publishing market (Greco, 2019; Monroe, 2007). After this acquisition, Bertelsmann CEO Reinhard Mohn had to negotiate with other major publishing houses. He also had to build working relationships with well-established Jewish publishers in New York who were uneasy with the market entry of a German company (see Chapter 1.1). Mohn connected with Oscar Dystel, the CEO of *Bantam* who was of Jewish descent, which helped mitigate these challenges to an extent (Berghoff, 2013, p. 182ff.).

In 1986, Bertelsmann bought *Doubleday Dell*. This resulted in the entity *Bantam Doubleday Dell*, which allowed Bertelsmann to

---

[1] We want to thank Rajeev Ravisankar, Ph.D. student in media studies at the University of Oregon, School of Journalism and Communication, for having co-authored this chapter.

"merge the logistics, distribution, and administration of its U.S. publishing and printing operations" (p. 184). The deal also put the company in a position that allowed it to set up contracts with authors for both hardcover and paperback. Bertelsmann made another significant move in 1998 when it purchased the widely known publisher *Random House*. The subsequent merger of *Random House* with *Bantam Doubleday Dell* allowed for the "integration of procurement, sales, and distribution" to create "tremendous economies of scale and scope" (p. 185). Having acquired *Random House* also brought major authors, such as Michael Crichton, John Grisham, and Toni Morrison (Reference for Business, 2021).

3.1.1 Regulatory Framework and Revolving Door Practices

The Telecommunications Act of 1996 came with major changes in deregulating media in the United States. It reduced the limits on national and local media ownership and loosened cross-media ownership restrictions (Price and Weinberg, 1996). This was a major shift in the U.S. media system. To politicians in favor of the act, it was the answer to the "need to support huge media entities that can compete internationally and contribute to a more favourable balance of payments" (p. 107). This goal outweighed any concerns "that minorities within the borders of the United States have their say" (p. 107) in media matters.

Deregulating measures did not apply evenly, however. The Communications Act of 1934 stayed intact and continued limiting foreign ownership in broadcasting "preventing RTL, for example, from running channels in the United States" (Berghoff, 2013, p. 174). Only in 2013, the Federal Communications Commission (FCC) began easing its approach to foreign ownership by allowing applications exceeding 25 percent ownership by foreign investors (Zakov, 2018). In 2016, the Foreign Ownership Order further consolidated the FCC's shift as it opened the door for requests of up to 100 percent foreign ownership (Zakov, 2018). In 2017, the FCC first approved an application for such ownership model of U.S.-based stations. This marked a substantial shift in its longstanding interpretation of ownership limits (Oxenford, 2017). Bertelsmann, like other big players, profited from this more general shift toward deregulation.

This relates closely to Bertelsmann's high-profile involvement in revolving door practices. Take the example of Joel Klein: The former head of the antitrust division in the U.S. Justice Department went on to become chairman and chief executive of the Bertelsmann U.S. operations. Klein was appointed to the Department of

Justice under President Bill Clinton's administration. He was involved in the U.S. government's antitrust case against *Microsoft* before resigning in September 2000. His appointment as head of Bertelsmann's U.S. operations came on the heels of the group gaining a stake in the file-sharing company *Napster*, which had come under legal trouble over copyright and distribution issues (Luening, 2001). At the time, Bertelsmann was looking to start a new service to exchange copyrighted songs via *Napster*. Klein was sought out not only to help the company deal with the hot issue of internet file sharing at the time and as to devise the company's approach to taking its media products online (Luening, 2001). Klein's role was to advise the company and then-CEO Thomas Middelhoff on legal and government issues as well as on prominent acquisitions. He was, for instance, expected to help deal with *BMG*'s proposed merger with the U.K.-based *EMI*, which faced significant regulatory challenges both in Europe and the United States (Oppelaar, 2001). Klein could do so because of his experiences in the U.S. Justice Department. Not only had he become close friends with Middelhoff, but his connections with European regulators were seen as potentially helpful in facilitating the *EMI* merger (Kirkpatrick, 2001). Insiders stated that Klein was "a key player in Middelhoff's plan to lobby the U.S. government to change foreign media ownership laws and allow Bertelsmann to acquire a U.S. television network" (Roxborough, 2002). The company's plans changed, however, following the attacks of September 11th and the ouster of Thomas Middelhoff as CEO, which marked the scaling back of Bertelsmann initiatives in the United States (Roxborough, 2002). In 2002, Klein left Bertelsmann to become chancellor of New York Public Schools.

3.1.2 Consumer Issues and Labor/Trade Union Responses

Bertelsmann, like other corporations, has tried to position itself as socially proactive on issues of racism and discrimination. In June 2020, more than 1,300 publishing industry workers in the United States initiated a day of action amid the Black Lives Matter movement. Participants in the action day highlighted their desire to "protest the industry's role in systemic racism" (Curto, 2020). This related to the lack of Black employees and authors as well as to substantial disparities between what non-Black and Black authors were paid as advances. In response, the company issued a statement expressing its stand against racism after the police killing of George Floyd and posted #BlackLives Matter on its website. It also drew attention to the planned action called "Blackout Tuesday" involving artists and employees in *BMG* (Bertelsmann, 2020). The company offers an online anti-racism class through Bertelsmann University, which is geared toward employees to engage with concepts of racial identity, privilege, and diversity (Bertelsmann University, n.d.). These types of programs have become common in the corporate world. Diversity consultants are invited to give workshops teaching individuals how race and other factors can play out in the workplace through microaggressions and implicit biases. While these trainings are generally a positive step in the right direction, they also come with the danger of drawing attention away from workplace power dynamics, such as institutional and systemic forms of discrimination, within larger structures of corporate power. With a few major corporations dominating the market, namely *Hachette, HarperCollins, Macmillan, Simon & Schuster,* and *Penguin Random House* (called the "Big Five") and with the near monopoly of retail sales by *Amazon*, this holds especially true for book publishing in the United States.

Thus, in response to Bertelsmann's 2.2 billion US-dollar-bid to purchase *Simon & Schuster* and merge it with *Penguin Random House* (see Chapter 2.2), a group of institutions and associations joined forces to call on the Biden Administration and the U.S. Department of Justice to block the deal (this included the *Authors Guild*, the *Open Markets Institute*, the *National Writers Union*, the *Horror Writers Association, Romance Writers of America, Western Writers of America,* and *Sisters in Crime*). They argued that if the purchase went through, it would lead to "more than half of key U.S. book markets under the control of a single corporation" (Lynn et al., 2021). In a letter addressed to Acting Assistant Attorney General for the Department of Justice Antitrust Division, the authors lamented the "horizontal expansion of power" by Bertelsmann. They argued that the proposed move would exceed limits articulated by Congress and the Supreme Court about the extent of control exerted by one company (Lynn et al., 2021).

This is particularly relevant since the Big Five publishers are facing two lawsuits – one related to price-fixing in the e-book market, the other related to price-fixing in the print book market. The first one is a combined class-action lawsuit on behalf of e-book consumers against alleged anti-competitive practices of the publishers and *Amazon*. The second one, filed by the same Seattle-based law firm *Hagens Berman*, argues that "the Big Five agree to anticompetitive restraints that prevent the Plaintiff [*Bookends and Beginnings*] and other booksellers from competing with Amazon" (Albanese, 2021a). This lawsuit, in particular, points to the use of "Most Favored Nation" clauses by *Amazon* with the big publishers. These clauses have "the intent and effect of controlling wholesale prices of print trade books and preventing competition with *Amazon* in the retail sale of print trade books" (Albanese, 2021a). Nina Barrett, owner of *Bookends and Beginnings*, explaining her motivation to join the case against the big players in publishing and retail sales, said: "Every single independent bookseller goes out every single day and fights a heartfelt battle to sell books ... against a ginormous competitor who has managed to accrue unfair advantage that we don't have, using tactics that are blatantly unfair" (Albanese, 2021b). In response, in September 2021, *Amazon* and the Big Five publishers filed separate motions seeking to have the federal court dismiss the class-action lawsuit. The companies asserted they did not have any agreements to fix prices and were not engaging in price discrimination under the Robinson-Patman Act, as alleged in the lawsuit (Albanese, 2021b). The publishers and *Amazon* also rejected the notion that agreements between them contained Most Favored Nations clauses amounting to an illegal price-fixing agreement (Arin, 2021).

In the meantime, Bertelsmann keeps on transforming its business in North America. In November 2020, *Berryville Graphics*, a Bertelsmann division, acquired *Quad/Graphics'* manufacturing facilities in Fairfield, Pennsylvania and Martinsburg, West Virginia. These were *Quad*'s last two units. They were added to the U.S.-portfolio of the *Bertelsmann Printing Group*, which also includes *Coral Graphics, Dynamic Graphics, Offset Paperback Manufacturing*, and *Digital Print Services* (Milliot, 2020). Prior to this acquisition, *Quad/Graphics* had garnered negative attention for unsafe working conditions and anti-union activities. 12-Hour shifts without breaks, workers being pushed to exhaustion, and low base pay, as well as a disregard for safety and environmental standards have been some issues described by *Quad* workers (Quad/Graphics worker, 2015).

Penguin Random House, on the other hand, keeps on moving facilities in search of cost reduction. In 2014, the publisher announced the closure of distribution centers in Pittston, Pennsylvania, and Kirkwood, New York, seeking to consolidate its operations to Westminster, Maryland, and Crawfordsville, Indiana. The move resulted in the loss of hundreds of jobs, including 286 jobs just in Kirkwood (Kelley, 2014). In August 2021, *Penguin Random House* announced the expansion of its distribution with new facilities in Hampstead, Maryland. Expecting to create 150 new jobs in the area, the distribution facility received a 325,000 US-dollars conditional loan through the Maryland Department of Commerce and a 25,000 US-dollars workforce training grant (Dieterle, 2021) (Table 3.1).

Table 3.1 Bertelsmann Subsidiaries in the United States (2020) (Bertelsmann, 2020)

---

3 Doors Productions, Inc., Reno
Alliant International University, Inc., Sacramento
American Idols Productions, Inc., Burbank
Amygdala Records, Inc., Burbank
Arist Education System Fund LP, Wilmington
Arist Education System LLC, Wilmington
Arvato Digital Services LLC, Wilmington
Arvato Entertainment LLC, Wilmington
Arvato Systems North America, Inc., Wilmington
Audigram Songs, Inc., Nashville
Berryville Graphics, Inc., Wilmington
Bertelsmann Accounting Services, Inc., Wilmington
Bertelsmann Digital Media Investments, Inc., Wilmington
Bertelsmann Education Services LLC, Wilmington
Bertelsmann Health and Human Science Education LLC, Wilmington
Bertelsmann Learning LLC, Wilmington
Bertelsmann PRH Finance, Inc., Wilmington
Bertelsmann Publishing Group, Inc., Wilmington
Bertelsmann Ventures, Inc., Wilmington
Bertelsmann, Inc., Wilmington
Big Balls LLC, Burbank
Big Break Productions, Inc., Burbank
Blue Orbit Productions, Inc., Burbank
BMG Audiovisual Productions LLC, Wilmington
BMG Production Music, Inc., New York
BMG Rights Management (US) LLC, Wilmington
Boostr, Inc., Wilmington
Coral Graphic Services, Inc., New York
DK Publishing LLC, Wilmington
Dynamic Graphic Engraving, Inc., Horsham
Eureka Productions LLC, Camden
FCB Productions, Inc., Burbank
Frederick Warne and Co. LLC, Wilmington
Fremantle International, Inc., New York
Fremantle Productions North America, Inc., Dover
Fremantle Productions, Inc., Burbank
FremantleMedia Latin America, Inc., Miami
FremantleMedia Licensing, Inc., New York
FremantleMedia North America, Inc., New York
Golden Treasures LLC, Wilmington
Good Games Live, Inc., Burbank
Haskell Studio Rentals, Inc., New York
HotChalk, Inc., Wilmington
Inception VR, Inc., Wilmington
Kickoff Productions, Inc., Burbank
Little Pond Television, Inc., Santa Monica
Mad Sweeney Productions, Inc., Burbank
Majorel USA, Inc., Wilmington

46 *The Global Media Giant*

Marathon Productions, Inc., Burbank
Max Post, Inc., Burbank
Mojiva, Inc., New York
Monashees Capital V, L.P., Wilmington
Music Box Library, Inc., Burbank
OCL Professional Education, Inc., Wilmington
Offset Paperback Mfrs., Inc., Wilmington
OP Services, Inc., Burbank
Original Productions, Inc., Burbank
P and P Productions, Inc., Delaware
Penguin Random House Grupo Editorial (USA) LLC, Wilmington
Penguin Random House LLC, Wilmington
PRH Holdings LLC, Wilmington
PRH Publications LLC, Wilmington
R and B Music LLC, Los Angeles
Random House Children's Entertainment LLC, Wilmington
Relias LLC, Wilmington
Rise Records, Inc., Salem
RTL AdConnect, Inc., Wilmington
RTL NY, Inc., Wilmington
RTL US Holding, Inc., Wilmington
Sasquatch Books LLC, Wilmington
SecuredTouch, Inc., Wilmington
SFLS, Inc., Wilmington
SND Films LLC, New York
SND USA, Inc., Wilmington
Sourcebooks LLC, Naperville
SpotX, Inc., Wilmington
Sputnik 84 LLC, New York
Stern Magazine Corp., New York
Studio Production Services, Inc., Burbank
StyleHaul, Inc., Wilmington
Synergis Education, Inc., Wilmington
TCF Productions, Inc., Burbank
Terrapin Productions, Inc., Burbank
The Immigrant LLC, Los Angeles
The Pet Collective LLC, Los Angeles
The Price Is Right Productions, Inc., Burbank
The Young Pope, Inc., New York
This is Hit, Inc., Nashville
Tick Tock Productions, Inc., Burbank
Tiny Riot, Inc., Dover
Triple Threat Productions, Inc., Burbank
Tundra Books of Northern New York, Inc., Plattsburgh
Udacity, Inc., Wilmington
University Ventures Fund I BeCo-Investment, L.P., New York
University Ventures Fund I, L.P., New York
University Ventures Fund II, L.P., Delaware
Vice Food LLC, Wilmington
VideoAmp, Inc., New York
Wanderlust Productions, Inc., Wilmington
Yospace, Inc., Wilmington

References

Albanese, A. (2021a, March 26). Amazon, big five publishers face yet another antitrust suit – from booksellers. *Publishers Weekly*. Retrieved from https://www.publishersweekly.com/pw/by-topic/industry-news/publisher-news/article/85909-amazon-big-five-publishers-face-yet-another-antitrust-suit-from-booksellers.html [January 10, 2022].

Albanese, A. (2021b, September 9). Publishers, Amazon move to dismiss booksellers' antitrust suit. *Publishers Weekly*. Retrieved from https://www.publishersweekly.com/pw/by-topic/industry-news/publisher-news/article/87324-publishers-amazon-move-to-dismiss-booksellers-antitrust-suit.html [February 15, 2022].

Arin, M. (2021, February 24). Most favored or too favored? Suits challenge MFN clauses used by Amazon and Valve. *American Bar Association*. Retrieved from https://www.americanbar.org/groups/business_law/publications/blt/2021/03/mfn-clauses/ [January 15, 2022].

Berghoff, H. (2013). Becoming global, staying local: the internationalization of Bertelsmann, 1962–2010. In Lubinski, C., Fear, J., and Perez, P.F. (Eds.), *Family Multinationals: Entrepreneurship, Governance, and Pathways to Internationalization*. Routledge. Retrieved from http://www.worldbhc.org/files/full%20program/A3_B3_FamilyMultinationals_BecomingGlobal_StayingLocal.pdf [January 9, 2022].

Bertelsmann (2020, June 9). There is no place for racism in our organization. Retrieved from https://www.bertelsmann.com/news-and-media/news/there-is-no-place-for-racism-in-our-organization.jsp [January 5, 2022].

Bertelsmann Annual Report. (2020). Retrieved from https://www.bertelsmann.de/media/investor-relations/einzelabschluesse/jahresabschluss-2020-bertelsmann-kgaa.pdf [February 5, 2022].

Bertelsmann University. (n.d.). Anti-racism – online course collection. Retrieved from https://www.bertelsmann-university.com/strategy-campus/program-information/anti-racism-online-course-collection.html [January 6, 2022].

Curto, J. (2020, June 8). Over 1,000 publishing workers strike to protest industry racism. *Vulture – New York Magazine*. Retrieved from https://www.vulture.com/2020/06/publishing-strike-racism-book-industry.html [January 25, 2022].

Dieterle, M. (2021, August 25). Penguin Random House to add 150 Maryland jobs with Hampstead distribution facility. *Baltimore Fishbowl*. Retrieved from https://baltimorefishbowl.com/stories/penguin-random-house-to-add-150-maryland-jobs-with-hampstead-distribution-center/ [February 5, 2022].

Drozdiak, W. (1998, May 13). Germany's media empire. *Washington Post*. Retrieved from https://www.washingtonpost.com/archive/politics/1998/05/13/germanys-media-empire/c0acb7e2-4785-4edb-b268-788e058cabbe/ [February 15, 2022].

Greco, A.N. (2019). The strategy of publishing. In Phillips, A.P., and Bhaskar, M. (Eds.), *The Oxford Handbook on Publishing* (pp. 190–205). Oxford

University Press. Retrieved from https://www.authorsguild.org/wp-content/uploads/2021/01/Bertelsmann-Letter-Final-2.pdf [February≈5, 2022].

Kelley, C. (2014, February 7). Penguin Random House announces closure of the Kirkwood and Pittston Warehouses. *Melville House.* Retrieved from https://www.mhpbooks.com/penguin-random-house-announces-closure-of-the-kirkwood-and-pittston-warehouses/ [January 16, 2022].

Kirkpatrick, D.D. (2001, February 1). Ex-regulator hired to advise Bertelsmann. *The New York Times.* Retrieved from https://advance-lexis-com.libproxy.uoregon.edu/api/document?collection=newsandid=urn:contentItem:4285-8VK0-0109-T1TJ-00000-00andcontext=1516831 [January 27, 2022].

Luening, E. (2001, January 30). Bertelsmann drafts antitrust sharpshooter Joel Klein. *ZDNet.* Retrieved from https://www.zdnet.com/article/bertelsmann-drafts-antitrust-sharpshooter-joel-klein/ [February 3, 2022].

Lynn, B., Rasenberger, M., Palisano, J., Moulton, C., Hasbrouck, E, Scantlebury, L, Kandle, T., and Wong, S. (2021, January 29). Letter to Richard Powers, Acting Assistant Attorney General Antitrust Division, Department of Justice. Retrieved from https://www.authorsguild.org/wp-content/uploads/2021/01/Bertelsmann-Letter-Final-2.pdf [February 1, 2022].

Milliot, J. (2020, November 3). Bertelsmann buys Quad's book printing plants. *Publishers Weekly.* Retrieved from https://www.publishersweekly.com/pw/by-topic/industry-news/industry-deals/article/84784-bertelsmann-buys-quad-s-book-printing-plants.html [February 13, 2022].

Monroe, M.H (2007). *The academic publishing industry: a story of merger and acquisition.* Retrieved from https://www.ulib.niu.edu/publishers/Bertelsmann.htm [January 16, 2022].

Oppelaar, J. (2001). Bertelsmann hire not so Klein cut. *Variety,* Vol. 381 (11), 4.

Oxenford, D. (2017, February 24). FCC approves for the first time 100% foreign ownership of US broadcast stations. Broadcast Law Blog. Retrieved from https://www.broadcastlawblog.com/2017/02/articles/fcc-approves-for-the-first-time-100-foreign-ownership-of-us-broadcast-stations/ [January 5, 2022].

Price, M., and Weinberg, J. (1996). The Telecommunications Act of 1996 and US Media Ownership. *University of Pennsylvania Scholarly Commons.* Retrieved from https://repository.upenn.edu/cgi/viewcontent.cgi?article=1759andcontext=asc_papers [January 30, 2022].

Quad/Graphics worker. (2015, May 26). Life has no dignity at Quad. *SocialistWorker.org.* Retrieved from https://socialistworker.org/2015/05/26/life-has-no-dignity-at-quad [January 18, 2022].

Reference for Business. (2021). *Bertelsmann A.G. – company profile, information, business description, history, background information on Bertelsmann A.G. Advameg, Inc.* Retrieved from https://www.referenceforbusiness.com/history2/76/Bertelsmann-A-G.html [January 18, 2022].

Roxborough, S. (2002, July 31). Bertelsmann readies self-review. New CEO mulls selling or revamping showbiz, media units. *The Hollywood Reporter.* https://advance-lexis-com.libproxy.uoregon.edu/api/document?collection=newsandid=urn:contentItem:46DF-F050-006P-R11S-00000-00andcontext=1516831 [January 26, 2022].

Zakov, D.A. (2018, September 26). United States: regulators open airwaves to increased foreign ownership. *mondaq.* Retrieved from https://www.mondaq.com/unitedstates/broadcasting-film-tv-radio/739718/regulators-open-airwaves-to-increased-foreign-ownership [January 10, 2022].

3.2 China: A Competitive Market in an International Context

For Bertelsmann, China belongs to the geographic region of "other countries", which makes for only 6 percent of its business activities. Still, the group considers the People's Republic of China (PRC), together with Brazil and India, to be an important growth region.[2] Thus, Bertelsmann has 24 subsidiaries in Brazil, 11 in India, and 30 in the PRC (Bertelsmann, 2020).

In his study on the involvement of Bertelsmann in China, Qianqiao Gu (2006) concludes that

> over a period of ten years, Bertelsmann has built a series of interlocking enterprises around its core book club operations, with patience, persistence and long-term thinking. Developing both content provision and sales capacity, it has attained a commanding position in the market.
>
> (p. 178)

Thus, Bertelsmann's business blueprints in China cover many areas, such as wholesale, retail, online sales, e-commerce, logistics, distribution, and management consulting. While in 2017, all Bertelsmann companies in China brought in a profit of about 12.5 million euros, in 2020, the annual profit fell to 8.76 million euros due to the trade conflicts between the United States and the PRC (Bertelsmann, 2020).[3]

---

2 We want to thank Kaifan Xie from the Tsinghua University in Beijing and Jingying Pan from the Shanghai International Studies University for having co-authored this chapter.

3 These numbers are relative, since not all Chinese Bertelsmann subsidiaries are wholly owned by the Bertelsmann Group.

Bertelsmann launched its first subsidiary in China back in 1992. Since then, it has successfully gained a foothold in the Chinese media market: *Fremantle Media* (*RTL Group*) has introduced successful TV shows such as "X-Factor," "Hole in the Wall," and "Take me out" to China (Bertelsmann, 2013, p. 45); *Random House* has distributed international bestsellers in China, and has sold the translation rights of its English-, German-, and Spanish-language books to Chinese publishers (Bertelsmann, 2012a); and *Gruner + Jahr* has published popular parenting, women's, men's and lifestyle magazines with its partner *Boda* (Bertelsmann, 2009a, p. 83). In 2006, Bertelsmann officially strengthened its presence in Asia by having built a new corporate center in China. This was also the company's first representative office in Asia (Reinke and Schurbohm-Ebneth, 2006, p. 94).

All of this happened in alliance with the many restrictive political guidelines in China. The Chinese government, partly in its attempt to protect its domestic market, strictly regulated the entry of foreign (media) corporations. With this, the Chinese government was not alone. In fact, many national economies have been trying to do so – in Western Europe, for example, France, with its "exception culturelle française," protects its cinema and film industry from uncontrolled access by U.S. corporations. In China, however, there have been strict regulations on direct investments of foreign (media) companies. For some time, this has caused tensions with foreign capital. While these tensions have somewhat been eased with China's accession to the World Trade Organization (WTO) in 2001, still only limited forms of cooperation were allowed. For instance, China's National Development and Reform Commission has had regulations allowing local governments to only handle foreign investments of less than 5 million US-dollars. A standard market practice for investments in China, therefore, have been the Variable Interest Entities (VIE) structures. These are contractual arrangements (e.g. for loans, operating agreements, consulting agreements, pledges) between foreign and domestic partners ensuring that the actual operator (or trustee) of a foreign media company is a domestic one. Though these VIE structures are currently changing, they have been a longstanding and reliable legal framework for investments from Western countries. According to Bertelsmann, also "some of Bertelsmann's activities in China are held by trustees ... for securing Bertelsmann's rights" (Bertelsmann Annual Report 2020, 2021, p. 37).

In contrast to many other Western companies, however, Bertelsmann managed to also secure the support from the Shanghai municipal government by means of long-term strategies: Already in 1995, Bertelsmann launched its first investments in China – in the usual Bertelsmann way – by means of a book club (*Bertelsmann Liber Stipes*). Though Chinese law at the time prohibited book *production* by foreign publishers, it did not prohibit end-customer *services*. This worked in favor of Bertelsmann. The book club distribution model had been unknown to the PRC (where book distribution was operated by *China Post*). *Bertelsmann Liber Stipes*, thus, introduced a new distribution model to the PRC delivering books directly to end-customers throughout the country. This meant that long before the e-commerce era, readers in remote areas of China had had access to books by means of home delivery services via Bertelsmann's book club model. Another way for Bertelsmann to circumvent Chinese regulations on foreign engagement was to establish the *Shanghai Bertelsmann Culture Industry Co. Ltd.* – a trading company for books, not a production company. Registered in the commercial registry of the Shanghai Industrial and Commercial Bureau, Bertelsmann distributes books from Chinese publishers via this company (Gu, 2006).

In February 1995, Bertelsmann also cleverly set up a joint venture with the *China Science and Technology Book Company*, a direct subsidiary of the Shanghai Press and Publication Bureau. This marked Bertelsmann's official entrance into the Chinese market (Tang, 2003, p. 381). One year later, *BMG* opened its Beijing office and signed famous Chinese artists, such as Sun Nan, who has since produced several music albums with a total circulation of 10 million copies, and Lin Yilun, also a pop star and TV actor (Li, 2003).

In December 2002, the General Administration of Press and Publication of the PRC adopted new measures for administering foreign book and newspaper distribution enterprises. This meant that as of May 2003, foreign enterprises and foreign publishing houses operating in China, including Bertelsmann, were given unprecedented opportunities and liberties (Table 3.2).

To broaden its sales channels, in December 2003, Bertelsmann bought a 40 percent share of the *Beijing 21st Century Samite Books Chain Co.* establishing the *Bertelsmann-21st Century Books Chain* with 17 outlets in Beijing (Zeng, 2003). However, book prices in China were much lower than those in European countries, while the rent on retail spaces in Beijing was almost the same. In consequence, profits of the Bertelsmann outlets were low (Zhao and Zhao, 2003) and 11 outlets closed again in 2006.

At the end of 2004, however, the Chinese book and newspaper market opened its doors to foreign investors for wholesale business, and Bertelsmann soon set up a joint venture with *Liaoning*

52 The Global Media Giant

Table 3.2 Bertelsmann Subsidiaries in the PRC (Bertelsmann, 2020)

Arvato Digital Services (Hangzhou) Co. Ltd., Hangzhou
Arvato Digital Services (Shanghai) Co. Ltd., Shanghai
Arvato Digital Services (Xiamen) Co. Ltd., Xiamen
Arvato Digital Services Limited, Hong Kong
Arvato Digital Technology (Shenzhen) Co. Ltd., Shenzhen
Arvato Logistics (Shenzhen) Co. Ltd., Shenzhen
Arvato Services (Nanchang) Co. Ltd., Nanchang
Arvato Services Hong Kong Limited, Tuen Mun
Arvato Supply Chain Management (Shanghai) Co. Ltd., Shanghai
Beijing 352 Environmental Protection Technology Co., Ltd., Beijing
Beijing Jianweizhizhu Business Consulting Co., Ltd., Beijing
Beijing Yi Jiu Pi E-commerce Co., Ltd., Beijing
Beijing Yiheng Chuangyuan Technology Co., Ltd., Beijing
Bertelsmann Equity Investment Fund Management (Shanghai) Co. Ltd., Shanghai
Bertelsmann Management (Guizhou) Co. Ltd., Guiyang
Bertelsmann Management (Shanghai) Co. Ltd., Shanghai
Bertelsmann-Arvato Commercial Services (Shanghai) Co. Ltd., Shanghai
BMG (Beijing) Music and Culture Co. Ltd., Beijing
BMG Rights Management (Hong Kong) Limited, Hong Kong
Boman (Beijing) Cultural Development Co. Ltd., Beijing
Fremantle (Shanghai) Culture Media Co. Ltd., Shanghai
Fremantle Productions Asia Ltd., Hong Kong
Majorel Hong Kong Limited, Hong Kong
Penguin Random House (Beijing) Culture Development Co. Ltd., Beijing
Penguin Random House (Hong Kong) Limited, Hong Kong
Relias Learning (Beijing) Consulting Co. Ltd., Beijing
Relias Online (Beijing) Consulting Co. Ltd., Beijing
Shanghai Bertelsmann Commercial Services Co. Ltd., Shanghai
Shanghai Bertelsmann-arvato Information Services Co. Ltd., Shanghai
Shanghai Kaichang information technology Co. Ltd., Shanghai

Publishing Group to establish *Liaoning-Bertelsmann Book Distribution Co.* (Shao, 2009, p. 7ff.). At the same time, Bertelsmann took advantage of the fact that China does not object to foreign investors cooperating with domestic publishers. The group, thus, cooperated with various domestic companies, such as the *Shanghai Science and Technology Publishing House* (to publish the *Journal of Car Fans*) or with *Liaoning Publishing Group* (to publish a series of books). In doing so, Bertelsmann built on its strengths and core competencies (Zhao and Zhao, 2003). In 2005, Bertelsmann also opened bookstores in *Wal-Mart* and *Carrefour* shops in China, hoping that the high customer traffic in these shops would bring new members to the book club.

In view of online book retailing, however, the book club model also had its day in the PRC. June 13, 2008 was a particularly black day in the history of Bertelsmann's book clubs in China. On that day, Bertelsmann announced the closure of its 38 bookstore chains across the country. The group responsible for its book clubs and BOL-business (Bertelsmann Online) was dissolved, and all executives left China. 18 days later, Bertelsmann also closed its 36 retail bookshops in 18 Chinese cities. While the club used to have 1.5 million members and was the largest membership-based retailer of books and other media in the PRC (Xu, 2008), a combination of factors, both in China and abroad, has seen the club wind up its operations (Table 3.3).

Table 3.3 Strength-Weakness Analysis for Bertelsmann's Entry into the Chinese Market (Lin, 2009)

Internal Conditions	Strengths	Weaknesses
	There is a great diversification of industrial products and services: books, film, TV, music, newspapers, foreign language products, new technologies, data services.	The group is conservative and slow in its decision-making processes (with the group being in the hands of one family).
	Bertelsmann's long track record and cultural heritage are strong and attractive factors for Chinese consumers.	In comparison and in contrast to the high degree of internationalization, the PRC lacks local market strategies.
External Conditions	Opportunities	Risks
	As the global economy and international trade continue to grow rapidly, there are good future opportunities for Bertelsmann in the PRC.	Due to an uneven and incomplete market penetration, there is a lack of local partners and content, resulting in slow market expansion.
	The growth of new markets in countries such as the PRC (and its accession to the WTO) opens up global market opportunities for Bertelsmann.	The rapid growth of competitors such as *News Corporation* (Rupert Murdoch) threatens Bertelsmann's activities in China.

In summary, Bertelsmann's strategy in China with its book clubs worked well for about ten years. After a low-profile entry into the market, Bertelsmann achieved remarkable growth rates. With beautiful mail-order catalogs and membership cards for key club members, Bertelsmann successfully catered to the mass tastes of Chinese consumers. During this early phase, Bertelsmann businesses basically revolved around its book clubs' activities. The group gradually formed long-term strategic investments, focusing on localization, globalization, and diversification of its business. Henceforth, it became a strong player in the Chinese publishing industry.

Bertelsmann's decline began with the rise of new competitors in publishing and in online book retailing. Selling books online was no longer about printing and packaging books, but it was about fast logistics and a new kind of price policy. The question whether this decline of Bertelsmann is related to the ownership structure of the group in the hands of one family, as Yihan Lin (2009) assumes, remains open. On the one hand, former CEO Thomas Middelhoff had failed precisely because of this issue (see Introduction). On the other hand, and regardless of ownership structures, Bertelsmann's activities in China show that the group has reacted far too slowly to the shift from a stationary to an online book market.

3.2.1 Successful Competitors and New Strategies of Bertelsmann

The arrival of the internet has had a negative impact on book clubs globally but especially in China. There are two competitors of Bertelsmann that show how one can conquer the Chinese book market successfully. First, there is the e-commerce company *China Dangdang Inc.*, known as *Dangdang*. It is a leading Chinese business-to-consumer company founded by Peggy Yu and Li Guoqing in 1999. In its beginnings, its niche market was limited to sales of traditional books and audio-visual products. Since 2001, however, *Dangdang* has turned into the busiest online book and audio-visual bookstore in China, similar to *Amazon* in the United States. In February 2004, *Dangdang.com* received 11 million US-dollars in investment from Julian Robertson's U.S. investment fund *Tiger Management*. By then, the company was well-positioned and strong enough to diversify its business. Subsequently,

Dangdang launched a periodicals channel and a fashion channel (Zhang, 2012). In 2016, *Dangdang* had more than 10 million registered customers per year and more than 100,000 sales daily (Basu and Wright, 2016, p. 180ff.). Its revenue in 2021 was about 1 billion US-dollars.

Bertelsmann's second very successful competitor in the PRC is the publishing group *Elsevier*, a member of the *RELX Group*, a global media group from Great Britain. As a specialist in online databases and with a worldwide dominance in the field of online journals in science, technology, and medicine, *Elsevier* entered the Chinese market in 2001. At the time, *Elsevier* kept a low profile. Its entry door into the market were schools whose supply of books was reserved for the largest Chinese bookstore chain *Xinhua* – a state monopoly with a total of 14,000 bookstores across China. With its low-price strategy, however, *Elsevier* managed to capture the schools: For a minimum subscription of 20,000 US-dollars per year, each school receives scientific journals of its choice, and for a further 30,000 US-dollars per year, each school receives a digital access to the online service *Science Direct* (Chen, Dong, and Zhang, 2013). By inviting schools to share their academic resources at such a low cost, *Elsevier* not only won over subscribers. It also developed a large readership that can no longer live without cutting-edge academic journals.

In the meantime, Bertelsmann is focusing on several growth strategies in the PRC: First and foremost, it supports and invests in creative companies. The group continuously supports Chinese start-up companies such as *DS Movie*, *Vue*, *Douban*, *Penguin Guide*, *Pencil News,* and *Mono*. Second, and probably the most important, Bertelsmann is highly active in the digital economy, that is, the development of e-books, digital reading platforms, and other e-products and e-services. For instance, Bertelsmann cooperates with the Chinese *Alibaba Group* by means of an alliance between the Internet-based e-commerce company *Alibaba* and Bertelsmann's music division *BMG*. The *Alibaba Group* comprises business-to-business online marketplaces, retail and payment platforms, and data-centric cloud computing services. It created a new live entertainment business unit under its *Digital Media and Entertainment Group* which focuses on ticketing, content creation, and live experiences. *BMG* signed a comprehensive distribution agreement with *Alibaba*'s digital entertainment unit aiming to develop a new business model for the Chinese entertainment market.

The deal covers the digital use of more than 2.5 million copyrights (Bertelsmann, 2015, p. 46).

A less successful venture for Bertelsmann in China was *Skoobe*, a platform launched in 2010 offering access to an unlimited amount of e-books for a flat rate. Since 2018, *Skoobe* has been a joint venture between the German publishing group *Holtzbrink*, the *Thalia* book chain (also from Germany), and Bertelsmann's two subsidiaries *Random House* and *Arvato*. *Skoobe*'s international success has not yet been repeated in the PRC.

A third new growth strategy for Bertelsmann in China is to focus on new digital companies. Through *Bertelsmann Asia Investments* (BAI), an investment firm founded in 2008, Bertelsmann has invested in more than 130 start-ups over the past ten years. Several of them are now listed on various stock exchanges. Among others, *BAI* owns a stake in one of China's largest music platforms *NetEase Cloud Music* (Bertelsmann, 2019a).

Not surprisingly, the equity of *Bertelsmann Equity Investment Fund Management* in China, responsible for *Bertelsmann Investments* in China, kept rising from 2014 and reached a peak in 2017. Though the company faced some difficulties in the following years, due to the trade conflict between China and the United States, and due to regulatory restrictions imposed by local authorities, the company's equity still maintained at a high level from 2018 to 2020 (Table 3.4).

Also, Bertelsmann's services company *Arvato* is playing an increasingly important role in China: *Arvato* is the group's highest-revenue subsidiary in China. It entered the Chinese market in 2001.

In 2009, *Arvato Services* started a joint venture in the Shenzhen Special Economic Zone in southern China, together with the domestic mobile communications providers and cell phone trading

Table 3.4 Bertelsmann Equity Investment Fund Management (Shanghai) (Bertelsmann, 2014–2020)

Business year	2014	2015	2016	2017	2018	2019	2020
Equity (T in euros)	1,148	1,309	2,021	2,099	1,557	1,926	2.011
Result (T in euros)	83	85	755	208	433	362	137

companies *Telling Group* and *Sinomaster Group*. *Arvato Services* holds 51 percent of the logistics center, which operates under the name *Arvato Logistics Services China Ltd.* The company's activities first focused on the distribution of cell phones for the two Chinese joint venture partners. Later, however, the company expanded its businesses. Currently, it provides logistics services to external business partners (e.g. warehouses and distribution networks) (Bertelsmann, 2009b).

Following the reorganization of the company's activities and its internal structures in 2011, *Arvato* has been operating at least 45 logistics centers delivering 100 million products annually (e.g. cell phones, accessories, and promotional materials) to more than 60,000 stores nationwide (Bertelsmann, 2012b, 2020). In early 2021, Arvato's supply chain and e-commerce services took over extensive logistics and fulfillment services for several new customers at different locations in China (Bertelsmann, 2021).

A study conducted at Dongha University in Shanghai in 2016 examined the job satisfaction of 150 employees of the Bertelsmann Group in China. As the survey results in Table 3.5 show, the findings were mixed: In general, symbolic satisfaction was higher than real satisfaction (Wang, 2016, pp. 34–51). Thus, in the highly competitive publishing and media industry in the PRC, Bertelsmann will have to step up its game (especially in terms of pay) if it wants to keep its workers.

Table 3.5 Job Satisfaction among Bertelsmann Employees in China (Wang, 2016)

Organizational Features	*Organizational Characteristics*	*Ranking (1 = strongly disagree to 5 = strongly agree)*
External Features	Pay and Bonuses	3.10
	Career Opportunities	2.53
	Company Work Place	3.48
Symbolic Features	Prestige	4.23
	Working Environment	3.67
	Openness for Innovations	3.05

References

Basu, R., and Wright, J. N. (2016). *Managing Global Supply Chains*. 2nd ed. New York: Routledge.
Bertelsmann. (2009a). *Jahresabschluss und Zusammengefasster Lagebericht*. Retrieved from http://www.bertelsmann.de/media/investor-relations/geschaeftsberichte/geschaeftsbericht-2009.pdf [March 9, 2022].
Bertelsmann. (2009b, February 24). Arvato Services gründet Joint Venture in China. Retrieved from https://www.bertelsmann.de/news-und-media/nachrichten/arvato-services-gruendet-joint-venture-in-china.jsp?atn=2862170&abp=2862170,2862222 [March 1, 2022].
Bertelsmann. (2012a, October 26). Bertelsmann treibt Wachstum in China voran. Retrieved from https://www.bertelsmann.de/news-und-media/nachrichten/bertelsmann-treibt-wachstum-in-china-voran.jsp?atn=2862170&abp=2862170,2862222 [September 3, 2022].
Bertelsmann. (2012b, September 10). Arvato liefert 100 Millionen Handys in China aus. Retrieved from https://www.bertelsmann.de/news-und-media/nachrichten/arvato-liefert-100-millionen-handys-in-china-aus.jsp?atn=2862170&abp=2862170,2862222, [March 1, 2022].
Bertelsmann. (2013). *Jahresabschluss und Zusammengefasster Lagebericht*. Retrieved from https://www.bertelsmann.de/media/investor-relations/geschaeftsberichte/bertelsmann-geschaeftsbericht-2013.pdf [March 9, 2022].
Bertelsmann. (2014). *Jahresabschluss und Zusammengefasster Lagebericht. Bertelsmann SE & Co. KGaA*, Gütersloh. Retrieved from https://www.bertelsmann.de/media/investor-relations/einzelabschluesse/jahresabschluss-2014-bertelsmann-se-und-co.kgaa.pdf [March 9, 2022].
Bertelsmann. (2015). *Jahresabschluss und Zusammengefasster Lagebericht*. Gütersloh. Retrieved from https://www.bertelsmann.de/media/investor-relations/geschaeftsberichte/geschaeftsbericht-2015-imageteil.pdf [March 9, 2022].
Bertelsmann. (2016). *Jahresabschluss und Zusammengefasster Lagebericht*. Gütersloh. Retrieved from https://www.bertelsmann.de/media/investor-relations/einzelabschluesse/jahresabschluss-2016-bertelsmann-se-und-co.kgaa.pdf [March 9, 2022].
Bertelsmann. (2017). *Jahresabschluss und Zusammengefasster Lagebericht*. Gütersloh. Retrieved from: https://www.bertelsmann.de/media/investor-relations/einzelabschluesse/jahresabschluss-2017-bertelsmann-se-und-co.kgaa.pdf [May 10, 2021]
Bertelsmann. (2018). *Jahresabschluss und Zusammengefasster Lagebericht*. Gütersloh. Retrieved from https://www.bertelsmann.de/media/investor-relations/einzelabschluesse/jahresabschluss-2018-bertelsmann-se-und-co.kgaa.pdf [May 13, 2022].
Bertelsmann. (2019a, January 7). Bertelsmann's investments in digital start-ups exceed one billion euros. Retrieved from https://www.bertelsmann.

com/news-and-media/news/bertelsmann-s-investments-in-digital-startups-exceed-one-billion-euros.jsp [March 1, 2022].

Bertelsmann. (2019b). *Jahresabschluss und Zusammengefasster Lagebericht*. Gütersloh. Retrieved from https://www.bertelsmann.de/media/investor-relations/einzelabschluesse/jahresabschluss-2019-bertelsmann-se-und-co.kgaa.pdf [May 13, 2021].

Bertelsmann. (2020). *Jahresabschluss und zusammengefasster Lagebericht*. Gütersloh. Retrieved from https://www.bertelsmann.de/media/investor-relations/einzelabschluesse/jahresabschluss-2020-bertelsmann-kgaa.pdf [March 1, 2022].

Bertelsmann. (2021, February 24). Arvato supply chain solutions grows in China. Retrieved from https://www.bertelsmann.com/news-and-media/news/arvato-supply-chain-solutions-grows-in-china.jsp [March 9, 2022].

Bertelsmann Annual Report 2020. (2021). Retrieved from https://www.bertelsmann.com/media/investor-relations/annual-reports/bertelsmann-annual-report-2020-finance-engl.pdf [January 20, 2022].

Chen, D., Dong, X., & Zhang, Y. (2013). A study of Elsevier's journal operating model and its digital publishing. *Science Technology & Publication*, Vol. 02, 10–14.

Gu, Q. (2006, January 1). Bertelsmann in China: low profile, patient growth. *Brill*. Retrieved from https://brill.com/view/journals/logo/17/4/article-p173_2.xml?ebody=previewpdf-49929 [January 20, 2022].

Li, S. (2003, March 6). Bertelsmann in Chinese style. *Life Week*. Retrieved from *http://www.lifeweek.com.cn/2003/0306/4862.shtml* [March 9, 2022].

Lin, Y. (2009). *The analysis of cases in Bertelsmann China Book Club and its significance*. MA thesis. Changsha/Hunan, China: Central South University.

Reinke, M., and Schurbohm-Ebneth, A. (2006). *Jahresabschluss und Zusammengefasster Lagebericht*. Retrieved from https://www.bertelsmann.de/media/investor-relations/geschaeftsberichte/geschaeftsbericht-2006.pdf [September 3, 2022].

Shao, T. (2009). *Research on Bertelsmann's exit from China*. Master's thesis. China: Henan University.

Tang, R. (2003). *Decoding International Media Groups*. Guangzhou: Nanfang Daily Publishing House.

Wang, Q. (2016). *Research on improving employer branding of Bertelsmann Arvato*. MA thesis. Shanghai/China: Donghua University.

Xu, Y. (2008, July 4). Termination of all operations in China, Bertelsmann finally says goodbye. *China News*. Retrieved from https://www.chinanews.com.cn/cj/cyzh/news/2008/07-04/1302095.shtml [March 9, 2022].

Zeng, Y. (2003, December 5). Bertelsmann enters Chinese book chain. *China Economic Times*. Retrieved from https://jjsb.cet.com.cn/show_105611.html [March 9, 2022].

Zhang, X. (2012). Marketing strategies for technology books in online bookstores – the case of Dangdang.com. *Publishing Research*, Vol. 5, 46–49.

Zhao, Y., and Zhao, C. (2003). Bertelsmann – the media giant leading the way for book clubs. *Science Technology & Publication*, Vol. 5, 55–59.

3.3 Latin America: "Export through Agents and Installation of Commercial Subsidiaries"

Since the 1960s, Bertelsmann has been exploring the Latin American market – initially as a kind of extension to its activities in fascist Spain.[4] Since then, Latin America has become a market in its own right. With its diverse activities, the Bertelsmann Group concentrates on the three major countries: Mexico, Brazil, and Argentina. However, the group's engagement spans over all of Latin America: *Penguin Random House*, headquartered in Barcelona, Spain, has publishing divisions in Mexico, Argentina, Colombia, Peru, Uruguay, and Chile. *Arvato, BMG* and *Bertelsmann Investments* are present in Brazil. *Majorel*, belonging to *Arvato*, has offices in Colombia and Peru, while the *Bertelsmann Printing Group* has a presence in Mexico (Bertelsmann, n.d.). Currently, Bertelsmann products appeal to 500 million Spanish speakers in Spain, Argentina, Chile, Colombia, Mexico, Peru, Uruguay, and Miami, where Bertelsmann has its own publishing headquarters for U.S. Hispanics (ABC Economía, 2017). It all started with books, however.

Spanish economist Maria Fernández Moya (2010) has summarized the process of foreign penetration of the Latin American book market by referring to the "Uppsala model." According to the model, international companies explored Latin America in "successive phases: specific exports, independent agents, installation of commercial subsidiaries and installation of productive subsidiaries" (p. 24). Other authors state that companies "choose to make the leap abroad to those markets that are psychologically and culturally closest to it" (p. 24, see also Cobo, 2000). Fernández Moya, however, concludes:

> As we are seeing, the early process of internationalization of Spanish publishing houses in the first decades of the 20th century perfectly fits the assumptions of the model established by the Uppsala School. Entrepreneurs chose foreign markets

---

4 We thank Daniela Inés Monje from the Universidad Nacional de Córdoba, Argentina, and Laura Diaz from the Universidad Nacional de Quilmes, Argentina, for the research assistance with this chapter.

close to the cultural and linguistic level, which, in the case of the publishing industry, made it possible to reduce the perception of entry risk and to market the same product as in the national market. At this stage, the process also meets the first two phases of the Uppsala model sequence: export through agents and installation of commercial subsidiaries.

(p. 33)

Thus, the leap abroad has less to do with cultural closeness but with risk management. The last step of the model, the installation of productive subsidiaries, either happens by founding subsidiary companies individually or by means of cooperating with local partners. According to Fernández Moya, "[t]his policy was followed by *Espasa Calpe, Gustavo Gili, Plaza y Janés, Santillana, Labor, Salvat, Océano, Aguilar, Bruguera, Alianza Editorial* and *Planeta*" (p. 37) – large publishing houses that used to be established in several countries in Latin America such as Mexico, Argentina, Colombia and Chile. Not surprisingly, similar patterns apply to all activities of Bertelsmann in Latin America.

In 2020, Bertelsmann's entrepreneurial activities focused on three major countries: Mexico, Argentina and Brazil, which happen to also be three major book countries. Mexico is the largest Spanish-language book market, with potentially 120 million readers, an estimated 200 book publishers and an annual production of around 20,000 books. Furthermore, it hosts an annual international book fair in Guadalajara. Similar dimensions apply to Argentina. Here, around 500 book publishers produce about 20,000 books per year, and the Buenos Aires Book Fair is an annual all-Latin American event. Brazil has around 800 book publishers, produces around 60,000 books per year and has around 4,000 bookstores across the nation. With such numbers, Brazil is the ninth-largest book market in the world (Wischenbart and Fleischhacker, 2020).

In 2017, *Penguin Random House* had about 8,500 authors and published more than 1,700 Spanish-language titles per year in nine countries: Spain, Portugal, Mexico, Colombia, Peru, Chile, Argentina, Uruguay, and the United States (ABC Economía, 2017). By 2020, through its subsidiary in Uruguay, the company was in control of around 40 percent of the Latin American book market (and it had its own distribution infrastructures). In Uruguay, 20 publishers accounted for about 56 percent of all titles published by the industry while only seven of them accounted for 90 percent of the overall turnover (Creative Industries Report, 2019, p. 5) (Table 3.6).

Table 3.6 Bertelsmann Subsidiaries in Latin America (2020) (Bertelsmann, 2020)

Argentina

Fremantle Productions Argentina S.A., Buenos Aires
Market Self S.A., Buenos Aires
Penguin Random House Grupo Editorial S.A., Buenos Aires
Grundy Productions S.A., Buenos Aires

Brazil

Affero Lab Participacoes S.A., Rio de Janeiro
Affero Tecnologia em Conhecimento Ltda., Sao Paulo
Arvato Participacoes Ltda., Sao Paulo
Arvato Servicos, Comercio e Industria Grafica Ltda., Sao Paulo
Bertelsmann Brasil Participacoes Ltda., Sao Paulo
Bico de Llacre editora de livros Ltda., Sao Paulo
BMG Rights Management Brasil Ltda., Sao Paulo
BR Education Ventures FIP
Brinque-Book Editora de Livros Ltda., Sao Paulo
Crescera Educacional II FIP, Rio de Janeiro
Editora Bonifacio Ltda., Sao Paulo
Editora Claro Enigma Ltda., Sao Paulo
Editora Fontanar Ltda., Rio de Janeiro
Editora Pequena Zahar Ltda., Rio de Janeiro
Editora Reviravolta Ltda., Sao Paulo
Editora Schwarcz S.A., Sao Paulo
Editora Zahar Ltda., Sao Paulo
Erste BBI Participacoes Ltda., Sao Paulo
Erste wv Fundo *de* Investimento Multimercado Credito Privado Investimento *no* Exterior, Rio de Janeiro
FremantleMedia Brazil Producao de Televisao Ltda., Sao Paulo
Intervalor Cobranca Gestao de Credito e Call Center Ltda., Sao Paulo
Intervalor Holding Ltda., Sao Paulo
Intervalor Promocao de Vendas Ltda., Osasco
SDS Editora de Livros Ltda., Sao Paulo
Stylehaul Brasil Agenciamento de Midia Ltda, Sao Paulo
FK LAB Tecnologias Educacionais S.A., Vila Olímpia, Sao Paulo

Chile

Market Self Chile SpA, Santiago de Chile
Penguin Random House Grupo Editorial, S.A., Santiago de Chile

Columbia

Distribuidora Penguin Random House S.A.S., Bogota
Majorel Colombia S.A.S., Bogota
Majorel Bucaramanga S.A.S., Floridablanca
Penguin Random House Grupo Editorial S.A.S., Bogota

Mexico

Alliant International University-Campus Mexico, S.C., Mexiko-Stadt
Arist Servicios Educativos, S. de R.L. de C.V., Mexiko-Stadt
Arvato de Mexico, S.A. de C.V., Mexiko-Stadt

FremantleMedia Mexico, S.A. de C.V., Mexiko-Stadt
FremantleMedia Services, S. de R.L. de C.V., Mexiko-Stadt
Grupo SL School of Medicine, S.A. de C.V., Mexiko-Stadt
Penguin Random House Grupo Editorial, S.A. de C.V.
Saint Luke School of Medicine, S.C., Mexiko-Stadt

Peru

Arvato Services S.A.C., Lima
Penguin Random House Grupo Editorial S.A., Miraflores, Lima

Uruguay

Ediciones B (Uruguay) S.A., Montevideo
Penguin Random House Grupo Editorial S.A., Montevideo

Venezuela

Ediciones B Venezuela, S.A., Caracas

As mentioned before, initially, Bertelsmann saw Latin America only as an extension to its general market expansion strategies, which took the group to Spain in 1962. At the time, the country was still under the fascist rule of Francisco Franco. Thus, there was systematic censorship of the press, film, and books, which included pre- and post-censorship; the state censorship office employed 30 people only for the monitoring of books. The works of Luther and Calvin were banned, as was *Tom Sawyer* by Mark Twain (cf. Salamon 2004). As the censors were mainly concerned with suppressing "immoral" books, however, the Bertelsmann Publishing House, with its popular reading material, had relatively little to fear for its *Circulo de Lectores* (reading circles). Apart from these *Circulo de Lectores*, Bertelsmann also owned the large printing house *Printer* in Barcelona and parts of the publishing house *Plaza y Janés* (Fernández Moya, 2010).[5] In 1982, when foreign investors were allowed to fully own Spanish companies, Bertelsmann acquired the rest of *Plaza y Janés*. According to Fernández Moya (2010), this "was a strategic step to be known throughout the Spanish-speaking market" (p. 80f.). Buying a "prestigious general publisher, with a strong presence in Latin America," enabled Bertelsmann to expand its "investment with the 1998 purchase of the Argentine *Editorial Sudamericana*" (p. 81). Thanks to this, Bertelsmann became one of the most powerful players in the Spanish (and eventually the Latin American) book market.

---

5 It is worth noting that *Printer*, operating much more cheaply than German printers due to lower wages and less strict health and safety regulations, was able to act as a price and strike breaker vis-à-vis printers in Germany.

Initially, in 1968, Bertelsmann used Spain as a springboard, first, to Venezuela and then, in 1969, to Colombia, Ecuador, and Mexico. The group first simply exported its products from Spain but soon built its own subsidiaries. In 1977, Bertelsmann opened the printing plant *Printer Colombia* – a joint venture with the newspaper and publishing group *El Tiempo*. The ownership of the Colombian print shop changed back and forth several times between Bertelsmann and the wealthy financial oligarchs of the Santos family who owned *El Tiempo*. However, *Printer Colombia* enabled Bertelsmann to go into in-house production locally and save on long distribution channels (i.e. Riaño, 2019; Fernández Moya, 2010; *El Tiempo*, 2007).

In 2010, the Spanish media group *Planeta* bought 50 percent of the *Círculo de Lectores de España*. The objective of this alliance was to strengthen its position in the face of digitization. By 2014, *Planeta* finally acquired the remaining 50 percent (Riaño, 2019). Similar to book analyses of the *Lesering* in Germany (see Chapter 1.2), also analyses of the *Círculo de Lectores* from the 1980s show a commercial bias. In addition, in Spain, 42 percent of all books came from Anglo-American countries, in the book club in Venezuela it was 37 percent and in Colombia 46 percent (see Becker 1985). Respectively, Gabriel García Márquez – journalist, writer, and winner of the Nobel Prize for Literature in 1982 – sharply criticized the *Círculo de Lectores* for its highly commercialized product range (García Márquez, 1981). Despite this criticism, the *Círculo de Lectores* continued until 2019. That year, *Planeta* – in the face of new types of competition such as *Amazon, ebay,* and *mercado libre* – ceased operations completely.

While, compared to the 1980s, the percentage of Ibero-American authors seems to have increased in the product range of Bertelsmann publishers in Latin America, the group's aggressive bestseller principle (see Chapter 3.1) is increasingly prevalent. Although important Latin American authors, such as Julio Cortázar (*Alfaguara* in Madrid) or Jorge Luis Borges (*Sudamericana* in Buenos Aires) are readily published, unknown, new, and young authors have hardly any chance with Bertelsmann's Latin American publishers (i.e. Román, 2015; Mudrovcic, 2001).

Since the purchase of the U.S. publisher *Random House* in 1998 and the subsequent merger with *Penguin* in 2013, creating *Penguin Random House* (see Chapter 2), the Bertelsmann Group, with 8,000 employees, is also the largest book publisher in Spain. In 2014, the group further acquired the Spanish publishing group *Santillana*, and in 2017, it purchased *Ediciones B* (a Spanish publisher with many

Latin American subsidiaries) and the Spanish comic series *Mortadelo y Filemón*. This comic series, which goes by the name *Mort and Phil* in English, first appeared in 1958 and has since reached a circulation of millions. To date, nearly 200 issues have been published in more than a dozen languages (ABC Economía, 2017). However, Bertelsmann is not only active in the three major Latin American markets, namely Brazil, Argentina, and Mexico, but also in the relatively small country Uruguay. Why? Uruguay has the highest percentage of readers in Latin America and with 6.5 titles per capita, Uruguay tops the Latin American ranking for the number of books published (Israel, 2020; Creative Industries Report, 2019).

3.3.1 A Media Service Giant in Latin America

Bertelsmann's large and powerful subsidiary *Arvato* is also active in Latin America. *Arvato* offers a wide range of services such as advising companies on IT, outsourcing strategies, buyer and customer management, supply chains, and financial investment strategies. In Colombia, *Arvato* has been operating a telephone call center with 600 employees for Spanish telephone and energy companies in the city of Floridablanca (population 267,538) since 2012. *Arvato* also has a call center in Buenos Aires with nearly 200 employees. This center generates annual sales in the amount of 11 million US-dollars (Dun and Bradstreet, n.d.). The company is also present in Brazil, the world's ninth-largest economy, where it offers supply chain management services for many customers in São Paulo.

In 2017, *Arvato Brasil* acquired a majority stake in the financial services provider *Intervalor*. Together with the Brazilian company *Cogna Eduçacão*, the world's largest private education group working exclusively for private schools and private universities, *Arvato Brasil* is heavily involved in the education business in Brazil. For instance, they have developed a program to collect outstanding semester fees from students (Bertelsmann, 2017, 2018, 2019).

According to Daniel Jones (1987, 1992), one conclusion that can be drawn from Bertelsmann's early activities in Spain and Latin America is that the group's global operations adapted well to culture and communication. While most transnational conglomerates – from *Springer* to *Bauer*, to *Condé Nast*, *Hachette*, or *Hersant* – mainly followed external growth strategies (by means of purchasing foreign companies), Bertelsmann's strategy had been different. Its entry into the Spanish market (with the exception of the printing industry) took place gradually. It merged with local partners, then used Spain as a venture point for Latin America (to better deal with cultural as well as fiscal and commercial issues) and, over the years, established itself in different markets. Eventually, the segmentation and concentration of the linguistic market made intermediate steps no longer necessary (Fernández Moya, 2009). However, Bertelsmann's activities in Latin America went beyond its core markets. Given the notoriously poor financial situation of state universities in Latin America, Bertelsmann has been at the forefront in establishing its own private-sector universities. This includes *Grupo SL School of Medicine, S.A. de C.V.* and *Saint Luke School of Medicine, S.C.* in Mexico City and *FK LAB Tecnologias Educacionais S.A.* in Vila Olímpia near São Paulo. For Bertelsmann, owning universities means nothing more than extending its value chains – its students have to buy and read company books. And to ensure that all potential students at a private Bertelsmann university are aware of their current and future social status, *FK LAB Tecnologias Educacionais S.A.* is located, not coincidentally, in the city of Vila Olímpia, one of São Paulo's most upscale neighborhoods. Also in Lima, Bertelsmann subsidiary *Penguin Random House Grupo Editorial S.A.* resides, not coincidentally, in Miraflores. This is the richest district of the Peruvian capital where the barricaded villas are guarded by private police and where millionaires like the Nobel Prize winner for literature and Bertelsmann author Mario Vargas Llosa live. Also in Ireland, Bertelsmann subsidiary *Arvato* is located in the decidedly posh Blanchardstown Corporate Park.

References

ABC Economía. (2017, September 25). Bertelsmann ya es la primera editorial mundial en castellano. Retrieved from https://www.abc.es/economia/abci-bertelsmann-primera-editorial-mundial-castellano-201709250136_noticia.html [February 1, 2022].
Becker, J. (1985). Der Bertelsmann-Konzern. In Prokop, D. (Ed.), *Medienforschung. Band 1: Konzerne, Macher, Kontrolleure* (pp. 48–82). Frankfurt: Fischer Taschenbuch.
Becker, J., and Bickel, S. (1992). *Datenbanken und Macht. Konfliktfelder und Handlungsräume.* Opladen: Westdeutscher Verlag, p. 107 ff.
Bertelsmann. (n.d.). Fact and Figures. Retrieved from: https://www.bertelsmann.com [November 1, 2020].
Bertelsmann. (2017). Bertelsmann achieves first-half operating group profit exceeding half-billion euros for the first time. Retrieved from https://www.bertelsmann.com/news-and-media/news/

bertelsmann-achieves-first-half-operating-group-profit-exceeding-half-billion-euros-for-the-first-time.jsp [February 1, 2022].
Bertelsmann. (2018). Bertelsmann strengthens its education business in Brazil. Retrieved from https://www.bertelsmann.com/news-and-media/news/bertelsmann-strengthens-its-education-business-in-brazil.jsp [February 1, 2022].
Bertelsmann. (2019). Back on the road to success with intervalor and Cogna. Retrieved from https://www.bertelsmann.com/corporate-responsibility/projects-worldwide/project/back-on-the-road-to-success-with-intervalor-and-cogna.jsp [February 1, 2022].
Bertelsmann. (2020). *Jahresabschluss und zusammengefasster Lagebricht.* Retrieved from https://www.bertelsmann.de/media/investor-relations/einzelabschluesse/jahresabschluss-2020-bertelsmann-kgaa.pdf [November 1, 2021].
Cobo, B. (2000). *Gustavo: Historia de Las Empresas Editoriales de América Latina, Siglo XX.* Bogotá: CERLALC.
Creative Industries Report. (2019). Promotion of investments, exports and country image. Editorial. Uruguay XXI. Retrieved from https://www.camaradellibro.com.uy/wp-content/uploads/2019/12/Informe-Industrias-Creativas-Editorial.pdf [February 12, 2022].
Dun and Bradstreet. (n.d.). Arvato Services, S.A. Retrieved from https://www.dnb.com/business-directory/company-profiles.arvato_services_sa.d646e32d57009d52576cfea156e44b29.html [November 1, 2021].
El Tiempo. (2007, July 26). Venden 50% del Círculo de Lectores. Retrieved from https://www.eltiempo.com/archivo/documento/MAM-2108209 [February 21, 2022].
Fernández Moya, M. (2009). Multinacionales del castellano. El proceso de internacionalización del sectoreditorial (1898–2008). *Revista de Historia Industrial*, Vol. 2 (2009), 23–50.
Fernández Moya, M. (2010). La lengua y la cultura como barreras de entrada: la inversión exterior en el sector editorial argentino, mexicano y español (1900–2009). *Anuario – Centro de Estudios Económicos de la Empresa y el Desarrollo*, Vol. 2, 41–93.
García Márquez, G. (1981, September 9). La desgracia de ser escritor joven. *El País.* https://elpais.com/diario/1981/09/09/opinion/368834412_850215.html [February 21, 2022].
Israel, S. (2020, February 16). Books in Uruguay, a small market with great readers. *The Country* (Uruguay). Retrieved from: https://www.elpais.com.uy/cultural/libros-uruguay-mercado-pequeno-grandes-lectores.html [February 12, 2022].
Jones, D. (1987). La penetracion transnacional en la cultura españiola: el liderazgo de Bertelsmann. *Telos (Madrid)*, Vol. 10 (1987), 125–142.
Jones, D. (1992). El papel de Bertelsmann en el mercado comunicativo español. *Análisi*, Vol. 14, 197–207.

Mudrovcic, M. E. (2001). Cultural policies in regional integration processes: the publishing sector in Mercosur. *Revista Iberoamericana*, Vol. LXVII (197), pp. 755–766.

Riaño, P. H. (2019, November 10). El fin del club de million de lectores. *El Pais*. Retrieved from https://elpais.com/cultura/2019/11/08/actualidad/1573200060_550763.html [February 11, 2022].

Román, V. (2015). Argentine publishing microenterprises and SMEs facing the challenge of the promotion, sale and distribution of books at the end of the 20th century and the beginning of the 21st. *Historia econômica & historia de Empresas*, Vol. 18 (2), 427–456.

Salamon, M. (2004). *Die Buchzensur unter Francisco Franco in Spanien*. München und Ravensburg: GRIN.

Wischenbart, R., and Fleischhacker, M.A. (2020). Global 50 The World Ranking of the Publishing Industry 2020. Ruediger Wischenbart Content and Consulting. Retrieved from https://www.wischenbart.com/upload/Global50_The_Ranking_of_the_Publishing_Industry_2020_MAF23Okt2020.pdf [February 12, 2022]

3.4 Non-Places

Financial markets, especially digital financial markets, are not bound by time or space, by geography or borders. In the context of globalization, they often work in "non-places" (*non-lieu* or *non-place*). According to the French anthropologist Marc Augé (1992), non-places are mono-functionally used areas without history, morality, culture or identity. Instead, there is a communicative neglect about them; they seem to not exist in real time. Companies that are making business in such non-places obey the principle of timeless opportunity. The purpose of non-places is to evade national or international legislation.

The existence of non-places is partially based on the unwillingness of the Paris-based Organization for Economic Co-operation and Development (OECD) to control global financial markets. Contrary to popular belief, the OECD's Financial Stability Forum (FSF) has neither been successful nor unsuccessful in combating corruption, money laundering, financial center stability, or tax evasion because it *cannot* regulate digital financial markets. Any such regulation would require challenging global capitalism as a systemic issue, and this would be a *contradictio in adiecto* (a contradiction in itself), meaning it would go against the pillars and purpose of the OECD itself (Deneault, 2012).

Tax havens are non-places. Used for tax evasion, money laundering, for concealing financial flows and for avoiding exchange controls, these financial havens are products of the Western colonial-capitalist system. Historically, within this system, top-rich elites have been in the business of defrauding states that simultaneously protect them (Ananyev, 2018). And while the legal, organizational, political and technical conditions that structure today's financial markets were developed in the centers of capitalism, that is, in the City of London, Switzerland and small monarchies like Luxembourg and Liechtenstein, the model of tax havens was later passed on to dozens of countries on the periphery, mainly in the Caribbeans (Harrington, 2016; Deneault, 2012). However, also the U.S. state of Delaware is a large corporate financial haven in. It is home to, among others, the U.S. arms and chemical group *Dupont*, and to *BlackRock*, the world's largest asset manager and shadow bank (Michel, 2021; Deneault, 2012). In Western Europe, one of the largest tax havens is the Isle of Man, located between Great Britain and Ireland. Legally, it does not belong to Great Britain but is directly under the British Crown.

There are numerous tax havens in the Caribbeans. These include: Anguilla, Antigua and Barbuda, Aruba, the Bahamas, the British Virgin Islands, the Cayman Islands, the Netherlands Antilles, St. Kitts and Nevis, St. Lucia, St. Vincent, and the Grenadines, and the Turks and Caicos Islands. The Bertelsmann Group is or was active in such tax havens, namely in Antigua and Barbuda, the Netherlands Antilles and the Cayman Islands. In the 2020 financial year alone, the Bertelsmann Group owned 26 companies in the Cayman Islands (Bertelsmann, 2020) (Table 3.7).

In the Cayman Islands, with only a few information disclosure requirements, the confidentiality of company information is very strict. This means, the identities of shareholders, the proportions of equity ownership, or the revenues of enterprises are, by law, strictly protected pieces of information. They cannot be accessed publicly, nor can a trust company disclose them at will (Deneault, 2012, p. 55ff.). If an enterprise needs to bring in foreign capital or overseas listings, it can first register an offshore company in the Cayman Islands, then acquire 100 percent of the equity of the domestic company, and finally submit the Cayman company to Hong Kong or the United States for listing in order to complete the overseas financing of the domestic company.

Table 3.7 Bertelsmann Subsidiary in the Caribbean (2020) (Bertelsmann, 2020)

Antigua and Barbuda
Grundy International Operations Ltd, St. John's Cayman Islands Aimint, Grand Cayman Agricultural Services Limited, Grand Cayman Buzzbit Inc. Gangwei Network Technology Inc., Grand Cayman Haizhi Holding Inc., Grand Cayman HLJK Information and Technology Cayman Inc., Grand Cayman Hooma Hooma Technology Limited, Grand Cayman INCAR Inc., Grand Cayman Know Box Limited, Grand Cayman Meixin Federation Group Inc. Mioji Group Limited, Grand Cayman Mi Ritao Inc., Grand Cayman moKredit Inc., Grand Cayman Penguin Guide Inc., Grand Cayman Qianye (Cayman) Ltd., Grand Cayman See Mobile Technology, Grand Cayman Tapai Inc., Grand Cayman The Look Limited, Grand Cayman TrendSutra Cayman Holdings Limited, Grand Cayman Velocious Technologies Inc., Grand Cayman Weplanter (Cayman) Limited, Grand Cayman Wothing (Cayman) Limited, Grand Cayman Wish Wood Holdings Limited, Grand Cayman Xianlife Limited Xiaobu Holdings Inc., Grand Cayman Zaozuo Zaohua ZWORKS Ltd., Grand Cayman

More than half of Bertelsmann's subsidiaries in the Cayman Islands have Chinese names, including: *Aimint, Gangwei Network Technology Inc., Haizhi Holding Inc., Hooma Hooma, Meixin Federation Group Inc., Mioji Group Limited, Ritao Inc., moKredit Inc, Qianye (Cayman) Ltd., Tapai Inc., Xianlife Limited, Xiaobu Holdings Inc.,* and *Zaozuo Zaohua ZWORKS Ltd.* (Bertelsmann, 2020). By means of these companies, Bertelsmann can circumvent the restrictions on foreign investment in the PRC (see Chapter 3.2). Here are some specific business areas of Chinese Bertelsmann subsidiaries: *Meixin Global* is a technology platform managing assets for high-end Chinese investors to help them facilitate legal and procedural aspects; *MoKredit Inc.* is a Hong Kong-based computer programming services company; *Tapai* is a platform to share short videos; *Velocious Technologies Inc.* is involved in computer software development and applications and is based in California; *Wish Wood Holdings* is a Hong Kong-based internet technology company; and *Xiaobu Holdings Ltd.* is a tech company involved in early childhood education and parenting for users in China.

White-collar criminals are prosecuted much more harshly in the PRC than in Western countries. For example, *Gangwei Network Technology Inc.*, operating in the Cayman Islands and with 18 percent Bertelsmann shares (Bertelsmann, 2020), was involved in a corruption case in 2017. Its former CEO was accused of misappropriating company funds from July 2014 until November 2016 amounting to about 10 million yuan. The company, headquartered in Hangzhou, China, is an e-commerce platform for steel providing services to steel mills, steel traders, and end users.

Bertelsmann, however, mostly coordinates its activities in the Cayman Islands by means of its subsidiary *Bertelsmann Asia Investments* (see Chapter 5). Not included in the list above is *Bertelsmann International Finance Ltd. N.V.*, which was founded by Bertelsmann in Curaçao in the Netherlands Antilles in 1977. The sole purpose of this bank was to handle the purchase of *Bantam* in the United States (see Chapter 2.2). After the successful takeover, the bank was closed. However, it has since reappeared in various Bertelsmann annual reports, only to disappear again a few years later.

3.4.1 Tax Havens in Europe and Arvato in Ireland

Within the European Union, Ireland stands out as a low-tax economy. This is the reason why Ireland is home to numerous large multinationals, led by such heavyweights as *Medtronic* (a medical technology company with annual sales of 30 billion US-dollars in 2020), *Shire* (a pharmaceutical company with annual sales of 15 billion US-dollars), and *Accenture* (a management consulting firm with annual sales of 39 billion US-dollars). The Bertelsmann Group is also prominently located in Ireland – although it does not appear, for instance, in the *Forbes Magazine* because it is not listed on the stock market. Still, in 2014, the Bertelsmann Group had two *Arvato* subsidiaries in Ireland. With a total of only 1,823 employees

72 The Global Media Giant

Table 3.8 The 14 Bertelsmann Branches with the Highest Number of Employees Worldwide (more than 1,000) (2015) (Orbis Database, 2017)

RTL Group, Luxembourg (11,011 employees)
Qualytel Teleservices, Spain (5,013 employees)
Gruner + Jahr, Germany (3,549 employees)
Courier direct service Dresden, Germany (3,274 employees)
Arvato Polska, Poland (2,835 employees)
ASF-Arvato Services France, France (2,398 employees)
Atresmedia Corporacion de Medios de Comunicación, Spain (2,042 employees)
Prinovis GmbH, Germany (2,000 employees)
Rudolf Augstein GmbH, Germany (1,467 employees)
Arvato Direct Services Wilhelmshaven, Germany (1,300 employees)
Arvato Finance Services, Ireland (1,261 employees)
Arvato Services, Romania (1,239 employees)
Prisma Media, France (1,089 employees)
The Random House Group, United Kingdom (1,069 employees)

(Bertelsmann, 2014, p. 43), they generated total revenues of at least 100 million US-dollars at the time (Table 3.8).

If one takes a comparative look at the relationship between national market size and the numbers of employees at Bertelsmann subsidiaries, it becomes clear that there is no consistent relationship between both. Bertelsmann subsidiaries have decidedly high employee numbers in small countries (e.g. Luxembourg or Ireland) and/or in Central European countries (e.g. Poland or Romania). These companies are, thus, producing either for export or they are enjoying major tax advantages.

In 2011, the *Irish Times* reported that in Ireland "Arvato Finance now handles more than 60 million transactions worth over €50 billion every year on behalf of its clients" (O'Brien, 2011). With operations in the UK, India, China, Brazil, the Philippines, and the United States, and with more than 60,000 employees in more than 270 subsidiaries across 35 countries, Andrea Kaminski, then president of international finance and *Arvato Ireland*, said "Our success over the past 15 years comes down to the partnerships we have established, not only with our international clients but also key organisations such as the IDA [Industrial Development Agency] and Chambers Ireland" (O'Brien, 2011). The close relationship between *Arvato* and public service institutions, not only in Ireland but across Europe, has since increased (see Chapter 2.4). *Arvato Ireland* profits from it.

According to various newspaper reports in the Irish press and on the *glassdoor* portal, however, working conditions at *Arvato* in Ireland appear to be difficult. Testimonials of former employees are not particularly positive. "I genuinely tried to think up one [good reason to work for *Arvato*] for a long time, however, I couldn't find any," one former worker writes (Glassdoor, n.d.):

> They facilitate a modernised sweat shop, numbers over people for these guys any day. The treat (free snacks, not hot lunch) is provided by their client we work for, not them. Though Arvato has the money, they will never offer a hot canteen for free, not even snacks. ... Moreover, it's all sugar to make you work harder, disguised as treats. People who worked here have grown fatter from stress and eating all those sugary and fatty foods, so it's really not a treat.
>
> (Glassdoor, n.d.)

Of course, there is no telling how representative these complaints from Irish *Arvato* employees are. A conclusive statement would require more throughout research, such as a content analysis of all comments as well as individual interviews with employees. Nevertheless, these complaints are not the exception, but they appear on a regular basis.

References

Ananyev, M. (2018). *Political Economy of Offshore Finance*. PhD Dissertation. University of California, Los Angeles.

Augé, M. (1992). *Non-Lieux. Introduction à une anthropologie de la surmodernité*. Paris: Le Seuil.

Bertelsmann. (2014). *Inside. The international magazine for Bertelsmann employees*, Juni, 2014.

Bertelsmann. (2020). *Bertelsmann SE and Co. KGaA: Jahresabschluss und zusammengefasster Lagebricht*, Gütersloh, December 31, 2020. https://www.bertelsmann.de/media/investor-relations/einzelabschluesse/jahresabschluss-2020-bertelsmann-kgaa.pdf (Abruf am 13. Dezember 2021).

Deneault, A. (2012). *Offshore Tax Havens and the Rule of Global Crime*. New York: New Press.

Glassdoor. (n.d.). See https://www.glassdoor.ie/Reviews/Employee-Review-Arvato-RVW14115331.htm (Abruf am 6. Dezember 2021).

Harrington, B. (2016). *Capital without Borders Wealth Managers and the One Percent.* Cambridge, MA: Harvard University Press.

Michel, C. (2021, November 19). The U.S. state of Delaware, on the other hand, is the largest current corporate financial haven in Western capitalism. *Foreign Policy.* Retrieved from https://docs.google.com/document/d/17sjZPhKVkOyxFyNrJNjO4sEpGtoRrqbHQJG_Stc9p9M/edit#

O'Brien, C. (2011, September 22). Arvato to create 150 more jobs over three years. *Irish Times.*

Orbis Database. (2017). Bertelsmann. *Bureau van Dijk.*

4 The Bertelsmann Foundation
"Making Politics"

The *Bertelsmann Stiftung* (Bertelsmann Foundation), founded by Reinhard Mohn in 1977, is the main owner of Bertelsmann Group. Although the foundation and the group formally are two separate entities, they are closely intertwined and both are controlled by the Mohn family. Aiming to influence politics and change society according to the ideas of Reinhard Mohn, the Bertelsmann Foundation has been using a wide variety of means to effectively promote the privatization of state sectors. Its projects focus on education, schools and universities, health care policies, demographic developments, labor and social policies, and foreign and security policies. In fact, there is hardly a topic in Germany in which the foundation does not have a say. Foundation and company experts, thus, effectively influence policies, laws, and reforms in the interests of the group and the family, not just in Germany but also in Europe and internationally. This chapter shows that the power of companies such as Bertelsmann does not lie in the market alone, but it lies in their influence on political decision-making (i.e. Bartsch, 2017; Buschow, 2012; Schuler, 2010).

The Bertelsmann Foundation is the central advocate pushing the interests of the Bertelsmann Group. The foundation is one of the most influential and well-networked neoliberal think-tanks in Germany (Pautz, 2008) with affiliate organizations worldwide, such as the *Bertelsmann Foundation North American* in Washington, D.C. or the *Fundación Bertelsmann* in Barcelona, Spain.

Although the Bertelsmann Foundation and the Bertelsmann Group are formally separate, they are closely intertwined by means of shareholdings and central stakeholders (Schuler, 2010). Also, both are controlled by the Mohn family. Criticism about the activities of the foundation flanking the globalization strategies of the media company has increased over recent years (e.g. Wernicke and Bultmann, 2010; Bauer, 2007), and scholars such as Thomas

DOI: 10.4324/9781003215608-5

76 The Bertelsmann Foundation: 'Making Politics'

Schuler (2011), have shown how "the foundation makes politics" (p. 1) largely in the interest of the company (also Schuler, 2010). Still, the heads of foundation play down the connections between both (e.g. in Thielen, 2012; Thunert, 2008).

The socio-political agenda of Germany (and consequently the European Union) is strongly influenced by the Bertelsmann Foundation. This relates to questions of privatizing public services, introducing tuition fees at German universities, deregulating the internet or German labor markets, changing unemployment policies or introducing welfare cuts, even global military interventions or German and European rearmament. There is almost no issue, the foundation is not concerned with (see Wernicke and Bultmann, 2010; Hantke, Pflüger, and Demba, 2010; Pautz, 2008; Biermann and Klönne, 2007; Barth, 2006; Schuler, 2004, 2010; Bennhold, 2002). Critics, such as former German politician Albrecht Müller, therefore, claim the Bertelsmann Foundation was "a state within the state" transporting its "neoliberal ideology into society" at large (Schumann, 2006).[1]

The Bertelsmann Foundation, founded by Reinhard Mohn in 1977 (see Chapter 1), is the main owner of Bertelsmann Group. According to Bertelsmann's corporate history, Mohn established the foundation to continue the family's social commitment and to ensure the long-term stability of the company (Bertelsmann, 2010). Jean-Mark Göttert (2001) even claims that the foundation was established because "[l]arge estates [e.g. companies] have to submit to the social obligation of ownership" (p. 36).[2] Reinhard Mohn "simply wants to use the experience he has gained as an entrepreneur over decades ... for the common good" (pp. 122 and 123).[3] However, according to Thomas Schuler (2010), not a sudden urge for charity led to the foundation's creation but it was a simple tax-saving strategy. Reinhard Mohn was keen on keeping as many capital assets as possible in the company. Mohn wrote: "The dominant objective that led to the establishment of this foundation was that the capital

---

1 Original: Die Bertelsmann-Stiftung sei "ein Staat im Staate", der sich "wie ein gefährlicherKrake" ausbreite und "die neoliberale Ideologie in die Gesellschaft" transportiere.
2 Original: "Große Vermögen haben sich der Sozialverpflichtung des Eigentums zu unterwerfen."
3 Original: "Er möchte ganz einfach seine Erfahrungen, die er als Unternehmer über Jahrzehnte bei sich und bei Bertelsmann gesammelt hat, zum Wohle der Allgemeinheit einsetzen."

assets could be brought in, thus ensuring business continuity by ensuring that the capital assets would then no longer be burdened by inheritance tax" (Gerstenberg, 2008). The foundation started with a capital of 100,000 Deutschmarks, and donations were initially written off. Later, though more and more of the company's shares were transferred to the foundation, Mohn still managed to maintain the impression of a non-profit status (Schuler, 2010). However, when Mohn, in 1993, transferred the majority of Bertelsmann's share capital to the foundation, he received widespread criticism. By means of this transfer, he had saved his wife Liz Mohn and his children Christoph and Brigitte a good 2 billion euros in inheritance and gift taxes. Further, because of the foundation and other legal structures, the Bertelsmann Group cannot be sold to third parties but remains in the hands of the Mohn family (Schuler, 2010; Schumann, 2006).

In 2018, the annual budget of the foundation was 70 million euros, and it employed more than 380 people working in Brussels, Washington, Barcelona, and in Gütersloh – in a glass building on the outskirts of the city right next to the corporate headquarters of the Bertelsmann Group (Munzinger, 2018). The foundation uses a wide variety of means to influence politics and change society according to the ideas of Reinhard Mohn. This means, it effectively promotes the privatization of state sectors and (market) competition at all levels, such as in higher education and in the healthcare sector (Volke, 2010; Schuler, 2010; Lohmann, 2010; Lieb, 2010). Simultaneously, it advocates more private civic engagement. For these purposes, the foundation has provided around 1.7 billion euros for different, self-defined projects since its inception (Bertelsmann Stiftung Annual Report 2020, 2021, p. 8). Not awarding grants or supporting third-party projects, its projects focus on education, schools and universities, health policies, demographic development, labor and social policies, and foreign and security policies (Schuler, 2010; Bethge, 2010; Biermann and Klönne, 2007; Barth, 2006). The foundation is so central to German and European politics that Frank-Walter Steinmeier, then president of Germany, in his greeting words for the foundation's 40th birthday publication wrote that: "If the Bertelsmann Foundation didn't exist ... we would urgently have to invent it" (Munzinger, 2018). Such estimate does not come out of nowhere. The foundation places its staff in central positions at the highest political levels in Berlin and Brussels (Schuler, 2010, p. 192ff.). Foundation and company experts, thus, effectively influence policies, laws, and reforms in the interests of the group and the

Mohn family (Schuler, 2010; Böckelmann and Fischler, 2004). This happens not just in Germany but also in Europe (Bartsch, 2017; Schulzki-Haddouti, 2010; Hantke, Pflüger, and Demba, 2010) and internationally (Oberansmayr, 2010).

4.1 Influencing Public Debates

Reinhard Mohn was convinced that it was possible to objectively measure the success and efficiency of any organization (Schuler, 2004). Thus, the Bertelsmann Foundation regularly compiles rankings of different institutions (Michalke, Naß, and Nitsche, 2010). This includes the well-known *Bertelsmann Transformation Index*, intended to measure the transition of states toward democracy and market economy (for criticism, see Wagner, 2010), and the *Benchmarking Project Office* (Projektbüro Benchmarking), which, in 1999, took Danish, Dutch and British labor market policies as "benchmarks" and called for a reduction of unemployment assistance in favor of subsidizing low-wage sectors in Germany (Eichhorst, Profit, and Thode, 2001, p. 28ff.). Another important ranking is the annual university ranking of the *Center for Higher Education Development* (Centrum für Hochschulentwicklung, CHE) for study programs in Germany. The *CHE* is an offshoot of the Bertelsmann Foundation (for criticism see Schuler, 2010, p. 168ff.; Bennhold, 2002).

Founded in 1994, the *CHE* sees itself as "an independent ... and internationally oriented think tank" and reform institution with convincing "good-practice" solutions (CHE, n.d.).[4] Its goal is a more competitive German and European higher education system. "As a neutral organization in the higher education system," *Bertelsmann Stiftung* (n.d.) claims, "CHE decides for itself which areas its work will focus on." Finding "new ways to free educational institutions from state regulation, overhaul internal structures and empower colleges and universities" in Germany and Europe, the *CHE* takes a "holistic approach" (Bertelsmann Stiftung, n.d.). Its critics, however, argue the *CHE* promoted a neoliberal transformation of the higher education system by lobbying media, politics, and society to increase acceptance of tuition fees and elite universities (Van Laak and Schulz, 2015; Barth, 2016; Schuler, 2010, p. 138ff.; Alidusti, 2010; Bennhold, 2002). *CHE* shareholders are the Bertelsmann

---

4 Original: "Wir verstehen uns seit unserer Gründung als unabhängiger, umsetzungsorientierter und international ausgerichteter Think Tank."

Foundation and the *Foundation for the Promotion of the German Rectors' Conference* (Stiftung zur Förderung der Hochschulrektorenkonferenz). One-third of the total three million euros *CHE* annual budget is paid by Bertelsmann (Bertelsmann Stiftung, n.d.). The Bertelsmann Foundation regularly influences public and political debates. For this, it either publishes its own studies or commissions others to do so. In fact, journalist Paul Munzinger (2018) claims that "studies come off the Gütersloh-ideas-assembly-line almost every week, with a sure sense of timing and a usual warning tone: child poverty is worsening, the tax system is unfair, Germany is missing out on digitization. The stuff of headlines." For instance, in October 2021, with rising economic tensions and trade conflicts between China and the United States, the Bertelsmann Foundation presented a study on what strategies German companies should use in the event of an escalation. It addressed different scenarios, such as German companies splitting into two parts, depending on their export interests to the United States or China. With such a split, the United States would not be able to threaten the "China part" of a German company with sanctions, the study said (Kronauer, 2021).

Hartwig Pautz's (2008) study on the reform of the German labor market, on the other hand, shows how the influence of the Bertelsmann Foundation mainly lay in providing concepts and "ideas which intellectually supported decision-makers' preferences" (p. 2). The foundation "helped with its readily available intellectual and organisational resources and played out its reputation of being a non-partisan and neutral agent of change" (p. 2). In short, it used its resources to help support developing policies outside the formal legislative process and civil service arena, and the German government gladly took up the offer.

4.1.1 *"Privatizing Politics"*

Bertelsmann studies are promoted widely. They attract considerable public attention and are repeatedly part of political debates in Germany and abroad. The *Benchmarking Project Office* study, for instance, found a widespread distribution in political and educational institutions (e.g. Eichhorst, 2002). The foundation, however, also initiates its own media campaigns, such as *You are Germany* (Du bist Deutschland) in 2005 – a campaign by German media companies to help improve attitudes toward the German economy. Coordinated by the Bertelsmann Foundation and supported by the advertising agencies *Jung von Matt/Alster* (creation) and *kempertrautmann* (strategic campaign development), the campaign was part of the *Partners for Innovation* initiative aiming to promote Germany as a viable and strong location for business and trade (Müller, 2005; Schröder, 2010).

Furthermore, the foundation facilitates events, for example, the *International Bertelsmann Forum* or the annual Bertelsmann party. Both help build direct long-term relationships with political decision-makers. Journalist Frank Böckelmann, the author of a book about the Bertelsmann Group, contends, however, that by connecting with politicians outside the parliaments and by making advance agreements with them, the foundation was pushing for "privatizing politics" (Schumann, 2006). Indeed, one of the foundation's papers even states that "it [the Bertelsmann Foundation] should also expand its ability to advise policymakers directly" (Bertelsmann Stiftung, 2002, p. 26). For this purpose, the foundation has created and/or supported several organizations in Germany. Next to the already mentioned *CHE*, this has included the *Center for Applied Policy Research* (Centrum für angewandte Politikforschung, CAP), the *Center for Hospital Management* (Centrum für Krankenhausmanagement, CKM) and the *Bertelsmann Science Foundation* (Bertelsmann Wissenschaftsstiftung). Each of these organizations has played a vital part in reforming the German educational and healthcare sector.

CAP is an extremely well-connected think tank for political consulting connected to the Ludwig-Maximilians-University (LMU) in Munich, Germany (Hänel, 2000). According to a *CAP* statement, the center aims to close the "gap between politics and research" (CAP, n.d.). Founded in 1995, *CAP*'s aim is "to bring together the privately funded practice-oriented research work attached to the professorship held by Prof. Werner Weidenfeld" (CAP, n.d.). Weidenfeld was a close advisor of former German chancellor Helmut Kohl, member of at least 14 national and international councils and working groups (Hänel, 2000) and, from 1992 to 2007, a member of the Bertelsmann Foundation Executive Board. In 2007, he was kicked off the board due to allegations of expense fraud; he had billed private entertainment receipts through the Bertelsmann Foundations. The proceedings were dropped in return for a 10,000 euros fine (Hägler, 2007). Still, *CAP* has been working with the Bertelsmann Foundation for several years, for instance, in publishing the *Bertelsmann Transformation Index*. With about 2.4 million euros per year, the foundation was by far *CAP*'s most important third-party funder (Bauer, 2007). It ended its funding in 2010.

Table 4.1 The Network of the Bertelsmann Foundation (Schuler, 2010, p. 192ff.; Bauer, 2007; Göttert, 2001, p. 122ff.)

Member of the Transatlantic Economic Council (TEC), the advisory body to the EU–US Free Trade Agreement (TTIP)
Member of the Transatlantic Policy Network (TPN) Member of Friends of Europe Supporter of the Atlantic Council Contacts to the American Institute for Contemporary German Studies (AICGS), USA Contacts to the Council on Foreign Relations (CFR), USA Contacts to the Transatlantic Community Foundation Network (TCFN), USA Contacts to the German Council on Foreign Relations (DGAP)

How closely the network of interest between policy work, business interests and research has been tied between different institutions connected to the Bertelsmann Foundation can best be seen in specific cases. Martin Bennhold (2002), for example, has written about Bertelsmann's influence on the reform of higher education in Germany in the late 1990s (see also Schuler, 2010, p. 138ff.). Bennhold (2002) concluded the reform was a "policy of submission" (p. 1) to the economic interests of Bertelsmann. A central figure in this reform was Werner Weidenfeld, the central research institute involved in the reform was *CAP*. This meant Bertelsmann's interests came full circle in working with government institutions. According to Bennhold, their cooperation amounted to a "downright institutionalized detachment of important planning and decision-making processes from the possibilities of democratic influence" (Bennhold, 2002, p. 5).[5]

---

[5] The network-like influence can be seen on a local level as well: For instance, thanks to extensive lobbying, *CHE* directly influenced education policy debates in the Higher Education Freedom Act in North Rhine-Westphalian (where Bertelsmann is headquartered) passed in 2006 (Van Laak and Schulz, 2015). In addition, in North Rhine-Westphalian, *Arvato* has been providing technical support for the state government's Service Center for years while Bertelsmann has received multi-million euros projects, such as *No Child Left Behind* (Kein Kind zurücklassen), inspired by George W. Bush's *No Child Left Behind* project (ultimately an educational fiasco) (Barth, 2016; Schuler, 2010, p. 160ff.)

It is worth mentioning that next to the foundation's efforts to influence public and political debates, also the Bertelsmann Group is heavily invested in lobbying in Europe and abroad (Table 4.1). In her study on the group's influence on media policy decisions in France, Marlen Bartsch (2017) shows that Bertelsmann has "a large media economic influence in France" (p. xx). "In particular, the subsidiary Groupe M6 has influenced media policy reforms through pronounced lobbying efforts vis-vis the Republican Party UMP" (p. xx). Politicians on the left lamented that the television station *M6* profited from lobbying efforts and personal relations with the French President benefiting from privileges made possible only by political connections. The actions of the Bertelsmann Group in France would, thus, destroy pluralism, media independence and culture. In contrast, conservative politicians, in favor of strengthening *M6*, argued the station needed to expand its international competitiveness (p. 223). Bertelsmann's business interests, thus, sparked several political debates in France.

References

Alidusti, K. (2010). Wie das CHE Inhalte stiftet – die »Politikberatung« der Bertelsmann Tochter. In Wernicke, J., and Bultmann, T. (Eds.), *Netzwerk der Macht – Bertelsmann. Der medial-politische Komplex aus Gütersloh* (pp. 195–213). Marburg: BdWi-Verlag.

Barth, T. (Ed.). (2006). *Bertelsmann: ein globales Medienimperium macht Politik; Expansion als Bildungsdienstleister und politische Einflussnahme-internationale Perspektive*. Hamburg: Anders-Verlag.

Barth, T. (2016, December 18). Lobbyismus: König Bertelsmann. *Heise Online*. Retrieved from https://www.heise.de/tp/features/Lobbyismus-Koenig-Bertelsmann-3572721.html?seite=all [October 16, 2021].

Bartsch, M. (2017). *Der Bertelsmann-Konzern und Die Französische Medienpolitik*. Wiesbaden: Springer VS.

Bauer, R. (2007, August). Global Player Bertelsmann. *Blätter für deutsche und internationale Politik*. Retrieved from https://www.blaetter.de/ausgabe/2007/august/global-player-bertelsmann [September 30, 2021].

Bennhold, M. (2002). Die Bertelsmann Stiftung, das CHE und die Hochschulreform: Politik der ´Reformen´ als Politik der Unterwerfung. In Lohmann, I., and Rilling, R. (Eds.), *Die verkaufte Bildung – Kritik und Kontroversen zur Kommerzialisierung von Schule, Weiterbildung, Erziehung und Wissenschaft* (pp. 279–299). Opladen: Leske + Budrich Verlag.

Bertelsmann. (2010). *175 Years of Bertelsmann–The Legacy for Our Future*. Bertelsmann, S. E. and Co. KGaA. Munich: Bertelsmann Verlag.

Bertelsmann Stiftung. (n.d.). *Centre for Higher Education*. Retrieved from https://www.bertelsmann-stiftung.de/en/about-us/what-weve-achieved/che-centre-for-higher-education [September 30, 2021].

Bertelsmann Stiftung. (2002). *Reformbilanz: 25 Jahre Bertelsmann Stiftung.* Gütersloh: Bertelsmann.
Bertelsmann Stiftung Annual Report 2020. (2021). Retrieved from https://www.bertelsmann-stiftung.de/de/publikationen/publikation/did/bertelsmann-stiftung-jahresbericht-2020-all [January 20, 2022].
Bethge, H. (2010). Bertelsmann macht Schule. In Wernicke, J., and Bultmann, T. (Eds.), *Netzwerk der Macht – Bertelsmann. Der medial-politische Komplex aus Gütersloh* (pp. 173–193). Marburg: BdWi-Verlag.
Biermann, W., and Klönne, A. (2007). *Agenda Bertelsmann. Ein Konzern stiftet Politik.* Köln: Pappy Rossa Verlag.
Böckelmann, F., and Fischler, H. (2004). *Bertelsmann: Hinter der Fassade des Medienimperiums.* Frankfurt am Main: Eichborn.
Buschow, C. (2012). *Strategische Institutionalisierung durch Medienorganisationen: der Fall des Leistungsschutzrechtes.* Köln: von Halem.
CAP. (n.d.). 25 Jahre CAP. Retrieved from https://www.cap-lmu.de/cap/ [September 30, 2021].
CHE. (n.d.). Über uns. Centrum für Hochschulentwicklung. Retrieved from https://www.che.de/ueber_uns/#1538663481205-7c99a147-928f [September 30, 2021].
Eichhorst, W. (2002, November 12). "Benchmarking Deutschland" – Wo stehen wir im internationalen Vergleich?. *Bundeszentrale für politische Bildung.* Retrieved from https://www.bpb.de/shop/zeitschriften/apuz/26610/benchmarking-deutschland-wo-stehen-wir-im-internationalen-vergleich/ [January 13, 2022].
Eichhorst, W., Profit, S., and Thode, E. (2001). *Benchmarking Deutschland: Arbeitsmarkt und Beschäftigung: Bericht der Arbeitsgruppe Benchmarking und der Bertelsmann Stiftung.* Berlin, Heidelberg: Springer-Verlag.
Gerstenberg, R. (2008, August 23). Nur im eigenen Interesse. *Deutschlandfunk.* Retrieved from https://www.deutschlandfunk.de/nur-im-eigenen-interesse-100.html [March 5, 2022].
Göttert, J.M. (2001). *Die Bertelsmann Methode: Die 10 Erfolgsgeheimnisse des vielseitigsten Medienunternehmens der Welt.* München: Redline.
Hägler, M. (2007, October 31). Abgang des Vorzeige-Bertelsmann. *taz-Archiv.* Retrieved from https://taz.de/!220824/ [September 29, 2021].
Hänel, B. (2000, April 19). Vordenker der Mächtigen. *CAP.* Retrieved from https://www.cap-lmu.de/aktuell/pressespiegel/2000/vordenker_der_maechtigen.php [September 30, 2021].
Hantke, M., Pflüger, T., and Demba, J. (2010). Der EU-Verfassungsvertrag und die Bertelsmann Stiftung. In Wernicke, J., and Bultmann, T. (Eds.), *Netzwerk der Macht – Bertelsmann. Der medial-politische Komplex aus Gütersloh* (pp. 447–453). Marburg: BdWi-Verlag.
Kronauer, J. (2021, November 16). Das Beste aus zwei Welten. *Junge Welt*, p. 3.
Lieb, W. (2010). Die »neue Freiheit« der NRW-Hochschulen: Freiheit für wen und wozu?. In Wernicke, J., and Bultmann, T. (Eds.), *Netzwerk der Macht – Bertelsmann. Der medial-politische Komplex aus Gütersloh* (pp. 215–227). Marburg: BdWi-Verlag.

Lohmann, I. (2010). Die »gute Regierung« des Bildungswesens: Bertelsmann Stiftung. In Wernicke, J., and Bultmann, T. (Eds.), *Netzwerk der Macht – Bertelsmann. Der medial-politische Komplex aus Gütersloh* (pp. 155–171). Marburg: BdWi-Verlag.

Michalke, M., Naß, O., and Nitsche, A. (2010). Mehr Humor und keine Katze – Rankingprodukte Marke Bertelsmann. In Wernicke, J., and Bultmann, T. (Eds.), *Netzwerk der Macht – Bertelsmann. Der medial-politische Komplex aus Gütersloh* (pp. 111–139). Marburg: BdWi-Verlag.

Müller, U. (2005, September 26). Ab heute bist Du Deutschland. *Lobby Control.* Retrieved from https://www.lobbycontrol.de/2005/09/bist-du-deutschland/ [February 12, 2022].

Munzinger, P. (2018, March 9). Eine Stiftung vermisst die Welt. *Süddeutsche Zeitung.* Retrieved from https://www.sueddeutsche.de/bildung/gesellschaft-und-politik-das-glashaus-1.3899280 [March 1, 2022].

Oberansmayr, G. (2010). »Get anywhere, fight anywhere, eat anywhere, stay anywhere« Bertelsmann finanziert Denkschmiede für die 'Supermacht Europa'. In Wernicke, J., and Bultmann, T. (Eds.), *Netzwerk der Macht – Bertelsmann. Der medial-politische Komplex aus Gütersloh* (pp. 455–462). Marburg: BdWi-Verlag.

Pautz, H. (2008). Think-tanks in Germany: the Bertelsmann Foundation's role in labour market reform. *Zeitschrift für Politikberatung,* Vol. 3 (4), 1–20. doi: 10.1007/s12392-008-0044-8

Schröder, S. (2010). Der Bertelsmann Konzern zwischen Politik und Öffentlichkeit: »Du bist Deutschland!« – Wer eigentlich? In Wernicke, J., and Bultmann, T. (Eds.), *Netzwerk der Macht – Bertelsmann. Der medial-politische Komplex aus Gütersloh* (pp. 141–153). Marburg: BdWi-Verlag.

Schuler, T. (2004). *Die Mohns: Vom Provinzbuchhändler zum Weltkonzern: Die Familie hinter Bertelsmann* (Vol. 61572). Frankfurt/New York: Campus Verlag

Schuler, T. (2010). *Bertelsmannrepublik Deutschland: Eine Stiftung macht Politik.* Frankfurt am Main: Campus Verlag.

Schuler, T. (2011, December 6). "Bertelsmann-Republik Deutschland" – Eine Stiftung macht Politik. Forum der Volkshochschule Solingen.

Schulzki-Haddouti, C. (2010). Auf in den Wilden Osten. In Wernicke, J., and Bultmann, T. (Eds.), *Netzwerk der Macht – Bertelsmann. Der medial-politische Komplex aus Gütersloh* (pp. 443–445). Marburg: BdWi-Verlag.

Schumann, H. (2006, September 25). Macht ohne Mandat. *Der Tagesspiegel.* Retrieved from https://www.tagesspiegel.de/zeitung/macht-ohne-mandat/755580.html [September 30, 2021].

Thielen, G. (2012, April 24). "Wir sind nicht die Speerspitze für die Bertelsmann AG". Frankfurter Allgemeine. Retrieved from https://www.faz.net/aktuell/wirtschaft/im-gespraech-gunter-thielen-wir-sind-nicht-die-speerspitze-fuer-die-bertelsmann-ag-11732788.html [October 13, 2021].

Thunert, M. (2008). Think Tank Corner. *Zeitschrift für Politikberatung (ZPB) / Policy Advice and Political Consulting*, Vol. 1 (2), 330–334. Retrieved from http://www.jstor.org/stable/24136534 [September 18, 2021].

Van Laak, C., and Schulz, B. (2015, July 3). Bertelsmann, Vodafone and Co. Wie Stiftungen die Bildungspolitik beeinflussen. *Deutschlandfunk*. Retrieved from https://www.deutschlandfunk.de/bertelsmann-vodafone-co-wie-stiftungen-die-bildungspolitik-100.html [September 30, 2021].

Volke, M. (2010). Das Konzept »Eigenverantwortung« und die Individualisierung der Gesundheitsprävention. In Wernicke, J., and Bultmann, T. (Eds.), *Netzwerk der Macht – Bertelsmann. Der medial-politische Komplex aus Gütersloh* (pp. 247–259). Marburg: BdWi-Verlag.

Wagner, A. (2010). Der Bertelsmann Transformation Index: Kapitalistische Marktwirtschaft als Projekt?. In Wernicke, J., and Bultmann, T. (Eds.), *Netzwerk der Macht – Bertelsmann. Der medial-politische Komplex aus Gütersloh* (pp. 463–469). Marburg: BdWi-Verlag.

Wernicke, J., and Bultmann, T. (Eds.) (2010). *Netzwerk der Macht – Bertelsmann. Der medial-politische Komplex aus Gütersloh*. Marburg: BdWi-Verlag.

4.2 Revolving Door Practices in Europe

Extensive revolving door practices involving the Bertelsmann Group (see Section "United States: A Top Market" in Chapter 3) have also taken place in the European context. In 2006, German journalist Wiebke Priehn studied how the political influence of the Bertelsmann Foundation plays out exactly. For this, she used the example of the German politician Elmar Brok – member of the Christian Democratic Union of Germany (CDU), chairman of the powerful Foreign Affairs Committee in the European Parliament and, from 2004 until 2011, manager of the Bertelsmann Group. Thus, Brok not only drew a salary from his work as a parliamentarian, but he also received a large salary from Bertelsmann (Priehn, 2006). During this time, he allegedly influenced numerous drafts and texts for the European Commission in the interests of Bertelsmann and put pressure on journalists who wanted to uncover such connections (see also Schuler, 2010, p. 201ff.; Hantke, Pflüger and Demba, 2010).

Also Martin Semayr, Secretary-General of the European Commission from 2018 until 2019, worked as a legal adviser and lobbyist for Bertelsmann from 2001 until 2004. During his time as a commissioner, Selmayr participated in several events organized by the Bertelsmann Foundation for the EU Commission, such as the

EU Citizens Dialogue (Karnitschnig, 2019). Also Aart Jan de Geus, former Minister of Labor and Social Affairs in the Netherlands and Deputy Secretary-General for the Organization for Economic Co-operation and Development (OECD), served as chairman and CEO of the Bertelsmann Foundation. The latter simultaneously and "quietly helped the Commission improve its public outreach" (Karnitschnig, 2019). Explaining the purpose of EU-related events coordinated by the foundation, De Geus stated that with "our [Bertelsmann's] ideas, concepts and other instruments we empower [European] decision-makers" (Karnitschnig, 2019). De Geus was both – an idea creator for Bertelmann and a European decision-maker. This was no exception. Bertelmann is at the forefront of sustaining personal relationships by means of regular invites and meetings. For instance, Jean-Claude Juncker, former President of the EU Commission, was invited by Liz Mohn to participate in an event at Bertelsmann's headquarters in Gütersloh to honor former UN Secretary-General Kofi Annan (Karnitschnig, 2019).

Another example is the Luxembourgish politician Viviane Reding – European Commissioner for Information Society and Media, from 2004 until 2010, and European Commissioner for Justice, Fundamental Rights and Citizenship, from 2010 until 2014 – who thereafter joined the Bertelsmann Foundation's board of trustees (Karnitschnig, 2019; Corporate Europe Observatory, 2014). The move was approved by the EU Commission while Reding was still a member of the European Parliament. The approval was based on the condition that she "avoided conflicts of interest" and "abstained from lobbying and defending the Foundation's interests to the commission" for 18 months after the position had ended (European Commission, 2014). The Bertelsmann Foundation, however, regularly reached out to Reding when she was European Commissioner. This included sending invitations to semi-private events, to executive training seminars, and to conferences on the future of Europe. The foundation also provided her with reports and other material on a range of policy and geopolitical issues (Cann, 2014). Reding spearheaded negotiations of the TTIP (see Chapter 4.3) (Corporate Europe Observatory, 2015). Another former member of the European Commission who also served on the board of trustees of the Bertelsmann Foundation is Benita Ferrero-Waldner. These examples only demonstrate the significant revolving door entanglements between the Bertelsmann Foundation and the European Commission. According to the Corporate Europe Observatory (2016), the foundation has been most effective in setting up consultations with European

Commission staff. Having also greatly increased its lobbying expenses, the foundation even started a summer academy with a role-playing game called "Lobbyism in the European Union" allowing participants to engage with lobbying experts (PlanPolitik, n.d.).

References

Cann, V. (2014). Former commissioner Viviane Reding and the Bertelsmann Foundation. *Ask the EU*. Retrieved from https://www.asktheeu.org/en/request/former_commissioner_viviane_redi_2#incoming-6496 [January 30, 2021].
Corporate Europe Observatory. (2014). Viviane Reding. Retrieved from https://corporateeurope.org/en/revolvingdoorwatch/cases/viviane-reding [February 13, 2021].
Corporate Europe Observatory. (2015, October 28). The revolving doors spin again. Retrieved from https://corporateeurope.org/en/revolving-doors/2015/10/revolving-doors-spin-again [February 3, 2021].
Corporate Europe Observatory. (2016, July 5). Thinking allowed? How think tanks facilitate corporate lobbying. Retrieved from https://corporateeurope.org/en/power-lobbies/2016/07/thinking-allowed [February 13, 2021].
European Commission. (2014, October 29). Procès-verbal de la 2103ème réunion de la Commission. Reference PV(2014)2103. Retrieved from https://ec.europa.eu/transparency/documents-register/detail?ref=PV(2014)2103andlang=en [December 10, 2021].
Hantke, M., Pflüger, T., and Demba, J. (2010). Der EU-Verfassungsvertrag und die Bertelsmann Stiftung. In Wernicke, J., and Bultmann, T. (Eds.), *Netzwerk der Macht – Bertelsmann. Der medial-politische Komplex aus Gütersloh* (pp. 447–453). Marburg: BdWi-Verlag.
Karnitschnig, M. (2019, May 22). How Europe's biggest media company infiltraded the EU. *Politico*. Retrieved from https://www.politico.eu/article/europe-inc-bertelsmann-business-philanthropy-politics/ [December 19, 2021].
PlanPolitik. (n.d.). Lobbyists are doing a job like any other, right? Retrieved from https://www.planpolitik.de/english/projekt/lobbyistinnen-machen-auch-nur-ihren-job-oder/ [December 10, 2021].
Priehn, W. (2006, December 8). EU-Parlaments-Hobbyist (CDU) bei Bertelsmann. *Themen: Bildung Globalisierung Kultur Medien*.
Schuler, T. (2010). *Bertelsmannrepublik Deutschland: Eine Stiftung macht Politik*. Frankfurt am Main: Campus Verlag.

4.3 The Transatlantic Trade and Investment Partnership (TTIP)

At the latest since its entry into the domestic U.S. market, the Bertelsmann Group has been a politically and economically highly influential player in transatlantic relations. In this role, it has been an active advocate of the Transatlantic Trade and Investment Partnership (TTIP) – a free trade agreement between the United States and the EU that was negotiated between 2013 and 2016. Both the Bertelsmann Group and the foundation were key institutions seeking to shape the policy discourse around the proposed agreement. Both were involved in advocating it and in getting it on the EU agenda by means of "behind the scenes prodding" (Karnitschnig, 2019). According to Matthew Karnitschnig (2019), the European Commission was "tacitly allying itself with corporate interests of the media giant that bankrolls it." In spite of these efforts, however, by 2019 the Commission stated that negotiations on the deal were "no longer relevant" (European Commission, 2019) partly due to massive public protests.

As shown above, the European Commission has had connections with Bertelsmann by means of revolving door practices but also by means of collaborations and overlapping interests. The Bertelsmann Foundation not only "actively supports the process of European integration by drafting recommendations" (Bertelsmann Foundation, 2019, p. 18). But in this role and with the support of the European Commission it promotes commission interests. For instance, it organized public events in the United States aimed at raising public awareness about TTIP. The foundation was, thus, 1 of 18 recipients of commissioned work intended to "advance trans-Atlantic cooperation through policy research and debate relevant to EU-US relations" (Cohen, 2014). Specifically, it was awarded a grant to carry out a "TTIP roadshow" to highlight the benefits of the free-trade deal for U.S. cities (Cohen, 2014). The TTIP Town Hall program received two-year support through the European Commission. Aiming at engaging with those "traditionally underrepresented in trade negotiations" (Bertelsmann Foundation, 2014), the foundation visited five states in the United States to hold town hall meetings – namely Birmingham and Mobile, Alabama; Los Angeles and San Diego, California; Boston, Massachusetts; Harrisburg and Philadelphia, Pennsylvania; and Austin and Dallas, Texas. For this, the foundation coordinated with the local chamber of commerce in Mobile, Alabama, with East Stroudsburg University, and the World Trade Center in Harrisburg, Pennsylvania (World Affairs Council – Dallas Fort Worth, 2014).

A key figure in these efforts was Anthony Silberfeld, the director of transatlantic relations at the Bertelsmann Foundation. Silberfeld extolled the benefits of TTIP at different occasions. Writing for the *Central Penn Business Journal* in 2014, he described the deal as a

The Bertelsmann Foundation: 'Making Politics' 89

"partnership of equals," through which the United States would gain access to a consumer market of 500 million Europeans. According to Silberfeld projection, U.S. imports to the EU would increase by more than 25 percent and lead to 750,000 more jobs in the United States. Highlighting TTIP benefits for Pennsylvania, a state in the "Rust Belt" with a history of heavy industrial production, he underlined that the trade deal was the only way to achieve economic growth in the region without additional government spending or budget cuts (Silberfeld, 2014).

The Bertelsmann Foundation partnered up with a range of entities to put together public TTIP events in the United States. University partnerships included an event with the McCain Institute at Arizona State University as well as with the Center for European Studies at the University of North Carolina. They also teamed up with World Affairs Councils and an EU Delegation as part of the 2014 "European Union Engage America Series" (World Affairs Council – Dallas Fort Worth, 2014). For the "TTIP and Fifty States: Jobs and Growth from Coast to Coast" report, the foundation collaborated further with the Atlantic Council and the British Embassy. In its foreword, Peter Westmacott (British Ambassador), Frederick Kempe (President and CEO of the Atlantic Council), and Annette Heuser (Bertelsmann Foundation Executive Director) highlighted that the trade deal would not only bring economic benefits. It would also serve as "a key strategic opportunity for the EU and the US" by sending "a powerful message to the rest of the world regarding transatlantic commitment to the development of global rules and standards" (Barker, Collett, and Workman, 2013, p. 3). The report emphasized that the deal would increase trade and investment, lead to job growth while retaining standards for the environment and product safety. The anticipated economic gains would be felt widely: A family of four in the United States would gain 865 US-dollars yearly while a European family would see an extra 720 US-dollars. Benefits would be felt across the United States, particularly in states with higher unemployment rates, while exports to Europe would increase. A state-by-state list of export gains and job growth identified California, Texas, New York, and Florida as those states most likely to profit (Barker, Collett, and Workman, 2013). The launch event for the report in September 2013 featured then-UK Deputy Prime Minister Nick Clegg, Senator Ron Johnson of Wisconsin, and Senator Chris Murphy of Connecticut (Federal News Service, 2013). At the event, Annette Heuser again pointed to TTIP labor market benefits as "greater exports lead to greater jobs" for regular people (Federal News Service, 2013).

References

Barker, T., Collett, A., and Workman, G. (2013). TTIP and the fifty states: jobs and growth from coast to coast. The Atlantic Council of the United States, the Bertelsmann Foundation, and the British Embassy in Washington. Retrieved from https://www.atlanticcouncil.org/wp-content/uploads/2013/09/TTIP_and_the_50_States_WEB.pdf [December 20, 2021].

Bertelsmann Foundation. (2014). TTIP town hall overview. Retrieved from https://web.archive.org/web/20171023082929/https://www.bfna.org/page/ttip-town-hall-program/overview [December 19, 2021].

Bertelsmann Foundation. (2019). Financial market integration in the EU: A practical inventory of benefits and hurdles in the Single Market. Retrieved from https://www.bertelsmann-stiftung.de/fileadmin/files/BSt/Publikationen/GrauePublikationen/EZ_Financial_Market_Integration_2019_ENG.pdf [July 27, 2022].

Cohen, A. (2014, January 13). Bertelsmann Foundation receives EU grant for "TTIP roadshow." *Bertelsmann Foundation*. Retrieved from https://web.archive.org/web/20190914101027/https://www.bfna.org/update/bertelsmann-foundation-receives-eu-grant-for-ttip-roadshow/ [January 28, 2022].

European Commission. (2019). Negotiations and agreements: the transatlantic trade and investment partnership. Retrieved from https://ec.europa.eu/trade/policy/in-focus/ttip/index_en.htm [January 28, 2022].

Federal News Service (Producer). (2013, September 24). TTIP and the fifty states. [Transcript]. Retrieved from https://www.atlanticcouncil.org/commentary/transcript/transcript-ttip-and-the-fifty-states/foundation-receives-eu-grant-for-ttip-roadshow/ [January 27, 2022].

Karnitschnig, M. (2019, May 22). How Europe's biggest media company infiltraded the EU. *Politico*. Retrieved from https://www.politico.eu/article/europe-inc-bertelsmann-business-philanthropy-politics/ [January 20, 2022].

Silberfeld, A. (2014, October 17). Transatlantic Trade and Investment Partnership a different kind of trade deal. *Central Penn Business Journal*. Retrieved from http://web.b.ebscohost.com/ehost/pdfviewer/pdfviewer?vid=4andsid=a0ee3c92-f1b4-4919-a31f-f441635b2218%40pdc-v-sessmgr02 [December 14, 2021]

World Affairs Council – Dallas Fort Worth. (2014, May 16). *TTIP Town Hall: the transatlantic trade and investment partnership and what it means for Texas*. Retrieved from https://www.dfwworld.org/events?cid=5andceid=2025andcerid=0andcdt=5%2F16%2F2014andcgid=1 [December 20, 2021].

5 Corporate Strategies

Having taken over the *RTL Group*, *Gruner + Jahr* and *Random House*, for years, Bertelsmann has pursued a typical corporate strategy – not innovative itself, the group has acquired and invested vast sums in new media and communications technologies of innovative market players that had proved successful. Next to strengthening its core businesses, Bertelsmann currently invests heavily in its digital transformation, in expanding growth platforms, and into growth regions, such as India or China. This chapter summarizes the analytical findings of the former chapters to bring light to Bertelsmann's broader corporate strategies.

The historical overview of the Bertelsmann Group has revealed four constituencies: (1) Since 1835, Bertelsmann has been owned by the same family. (2) The Bertelsmann Group has always had rights of co-determination and participatory approaches for its employees (Göttert, 2001). The reason: Reinhard Mohn was inventive when it came to keeping capital assets in the company. In order to save money on taxes and social security, he introduced a profit-sharing scheme for his employees in the early 1970s. This earned Mohn the less than appropriate nickname "red poppy" (Gerstenberg, 2008). In consequence, since 1970, the Bertelsmann Media Group has practiced indirect participation via an asset management company (*Vermögensverwaltungs-Gesellschaft*, VVG). The *VVG* invested the capital accumulated by means of profit-sharing, and Bertelsmann employees participated in VVG profits and losses as silent partners.

This profit-sharing model (though changed) is still in place today. In 2020, Bertelsmann employees received a total of 88 million euros in profit-sharing and bonuses (the previous year, it had been 96 million euros) (Bertelsmann Annual Report 2020, 2021, p. 80). While these participatory models might seem socially innovative, they can also be considered deeply anti-unionist. They are not based on a conflict model of diverging interests between employer and

DOI: 10.4324/9781003215608-6

employees, but they push an ideology of "we're in this together", hindering the formation and expression of common workers' interests. For instance, in a video message, Liz Mohn addressed the group's top management and more than 130,000 employees worldwide. Referring to the Covid-19 pandemic, she stressed: "Bertelsmann and all of you have shown that we can deal with a global crisis. By looking out for each other and providing protection. It's thanks to your hard work and skill that Bertelsmann is doing so well today" (Börsenblatt, 2021). At the same time, in the first quarter of 2021, the actual Bertelsmann Group profit share of around 30 million euros was distributed to a good 18,000 employees exclusively located in Germany, though its amount was linked to the group's global success (and its 130,000 employees). Since April 2021, however, the group has been working on switching to a divisional profit-sharing model (Bertelsmann, 2021). (3) The contents published by the Bertelsmann Group are overall popular or populist and/or oriented to mainstream tastes. (4) With the building of distribution channels (first, for Christian reading circles, then for the German *Wehrmacht*, followed by the Bertelsmann *Lesering*), the Bertelsmann Group is a specialist in developing secure sales channels (and their respective infrastructures) beyond the stationary book trade. With a priority focus on sales over content, the group has spent decades building an in-depth system or organization and systematization. This would be impossible without the collected data of demographics, places of residence, and the socio-cultural and regional backgrounds of its readers (including addresses, street directories, subscription management, etc.) (Becker, 1985a, 1985b). Thus, with long-term experience and know-how as well as the readily available infrastructures in its service, the group was able to make a successful leap into the world of digital services – they were, at first, transferred to the now defunct *DirectGroup*, and then to the new *Arvato* services division.

In the 1950s, Bertelsmann founded the extremely successful Bertelsmann book club. This was a key moment in discussions about new book markets. However, for Bertelsmann, not the *medium* (the book) was important but it was the handling of new sales and distribution *infrastructures*. Since the 1950s, Bertelsmann has been active as a service company. For example, it took over the delivery of books for other publishers. For Bertelsmann, it was, thus, less about books than about the logistics and new technologies behind their distribution. To this day, the group has remained true to this line of business. With its dual strategy – growth abroad and making use of new technologies – Bertelsmann has become a large provider of intangible products. Thus, one of the group's major growth markets is global services (for global supply chains, financial flows, IT systems, and customer communications).

For years, Bertelsmann has pursued another typical corporate strategy: the group has not been innovative itself but it invested vast sums in new media and communications technologies of innovative market players (see Becker, 2017; Becker and Bickel, 1992). This could be said for the involvement of Bertelsmann in all media markets (music, services, etc.), and for the strategies of other global players in (digital) media and communication markets such as *Amazon* or *Alphabet* (i.e. Brevini and Swiatek, 2020; Lee, 2019). Due to their significant influence on global communication and services, the strategy of the Bertelsmann Group has shifted. Next to strengthening its core businesses, Bertelsmann invests heavily in digital communication (including IT, finances, and services) and in expanding growth platforms, as well as in growth regions, such as Brazil, India, or China (Bertelsmann Annual Report 2020, 2021, p. 5).

This strategy becomes manifest in *Bertelsmann Investments* – the group's global venture capital division. It comprises four funds: *Bertelsmann Asia Investments, Bertelsmann India Investments, Bertelsmann Brazil Investments,* and *Bertelsmann Digital Media Investments* (BDMI) with a focus on the United States and Europe. *Bertelsmann Investments* also invests in selected funds in Southeast Asia and Africa, among others, and in funds with a focus on new technologies. By 2022, *Bertelsmann Investments* has invested over 1 billion euros in more than 250 companies and funds. This often includes start-ups in media, services, and education, often with a focus on emerging technologies. The Bertelsmann Investments Digital Partners initiative aims to enable collaboration between these start-ups to further advance the digitization of the group's business (Bertelsmann, n.d.-a, n.d.-b).

Further, the activities of Bertelsmann suggest a broad range of financial activities around the globe. For instance, Bertelsmann subsidiaries in Brazil, such as *Erste wv Fundo de Investimento Multimercado Credito Privado Investimento no Exterior* in Rio de Janeiro or *Intervalor Promocao de Vendas Ltda.* in Osasco, are first and foremost investment funds or bank-like financial service providers. This shift in focus makes sense financially. Generally, the returns in the financial services sector are much higher than in the book market. It is a risky business, however.

Also, the group's engagement in media sectors around the world is not without issues. In China, with its 4,600 employees, the group is well placed to make profits whenever it is not a question of content but of distribution and infrastructures. However, tensions between the German capital and Chinese content persist, and they will likely determine Bertelsmann's future in the region. As long as China's regulations prohibit foreign publishers and media corporations from producing their own content, Bertelsmann's involvement in the PRC will remain difficult and fragile (Gu, 2006).

For Bertelsmann's subsidiaries in Latin America, on the other hand, local content means little more than distributing international bestsellers, especially from the United States. In a deregulated world market, local content contradicts the exploitation of mass markets. The Bertelsmann Group, therefore, currently pushes forward the idea of creating "national media champions." They are to "form a potential counterweight to the major US tech groups in their respective markets" by means of "internationally exploitable media content" (movies, series, and shows to books and music) (Bertelsmann, n.d.-b). The question of content production, thus, lays open the group's search for new business strategies. This also applies to the online education market.

In 2020, only 25.3 percent of the Bertelsmann Group's revenues came from tangible goods (Bertelsmann, 2020, p. 68) – the ratio between tangible and intangible goods has changed completely over the last decades and will likely continue to do so. However, it is important to keep in mind that large corporations by and in themselves *cannot* be innovative: they simply are too large, too confusing, and structurally incapable of tying together all their individual parts. This is why large corporations such as Bertelsmann experience very expensive frictional losses. If one compares, for instance, the industrial manufacturing conglomerate *Siemens* with *Bertelsmann*, one finds very different corporate strategies: *Siemens* gets rid of its unprofitable parts every year. It sells them or converts them into independent companies. Bertelsmann (similar to *Amazon, Apple,* or *Meta*), on the other hand, constantly buys up other companies, absorbs them and grows on their innovations. Different from *Amazon, Apple,* or *Meta*, Bertelsmann is not listed on the stock market, however, which makes it harder for the group to receive loans (e.g. for further investments). It is also not one of the Fortune's 100 largest corporations, a list that comprises the world's largest companies by revenue. On the other hand, the Bertelsmann Group is under the control of a family, not shareholders. This also means that Bertelsmann is well protected against hostile takeovers.

References

Becker, J. (1985a). Activities in foreign countries and new technologies of a transnational corporation: the example of Bertelsmann. *Media, Culture and Society*, Vol. 7 (3), 313–330. doi: 10.1177/016344385007003004

Becker, J. (1985b). Ein multinationaler Informationskonzern angesichts neuer Technologien: Bertelsmann. In Mettler, P.H. (Ed.), *Wohin expandieren Multinationale Konzerne?* (pp. 24–41). Frankfurt: Haag and Herchen Verlag.

Becker, J., and Bickel, S. (1992). *Datenbanken und Macht. Konfliktfelder und Handlungsräume*. Opladen: Westdeutscher Verlag, p. 107ff.

Bertelsmann. (n.d.-a). Bertelsmann Investments. Retrieved from https://www.bertelsmann.de/bereiche/bertelsmann-investments/#st-1 [February 27, 2022].

Bertelsmann. (n.d.-b). Strategy. Retrieved from https://www.bertelsmann.de/bereiche/rtl-group/#st-1 [January 30, 2022]. https://www.bertelsmann.com/company/strategy/

Bertelsmann. (2020). *Jahresabschluss und zusammengefasster Lagebericht*. Gütersloh. Retrieved from https://www.bertelsmann.de/media/investor-relations/einzelabschluesse/jahresabschluss-2020-bertelsmann-kgaa.pdf [March 1, 2022].

Bertelsmann Annual Report 2020. (2021). Retrieved from https://www.bertelsmann.com/media/investor-relations/annual-reports/bertelsmann-annual-report-2020-finance-engl.pdf [January 20, 2022].

Börsenblatt. (2021, April 2021). Bertelsmann setzt neue strategische Prioritäten. *Börsenblatt*. Retrieved from https://www.boersenblatt.net/news/verlage-news/bertelsmann-setzt-neue-strategische-prioritaeten-175131 [January 5, 2022].

Brevini, B., and Swiatek, L. (2020). *Amazon Understanding a Global Communication Giant. Global Media Giants*. New York: Routledge.

Gerstenberg, R. (2008, August 23). Nur im eigenen Interesse. *Deutschlandfunk*. Retrieved from https://www.deutschlandfunk.de/nur-im-eigenen-interesse-100.html [March 5, 2022].

Göttert, J.M. (2001). Die Bertelsmann Methode: Die 10 Erfolgsgeheimnisse des vielseitigsten Medienunternehmens der Welt. München: Redline.

Gu, Q. (2006, January 1). Bertelsmann in China: low profile, patient growth. *Brill*. Retrieved from https://brill.com/view/journals/logo/17/4/article-p173_2.xml?ebody=previewpdf-49929 [January 20, 2022].

Lee, M. (2019). *Alphabet the Becoming of Google. Global Media Giants*. New York: Routledge.

Concluding Remarks
A Transnational Information and Service Giant

The day Thomas Schuler published his book *Bertelsmann's Republic of Germany – A Foundation Makes Politics* (Bertelsmannrepublik Deutschland – eine Stiftung macht Politik) in 2010, the Bertelsmann Group published a responding statement. In it, Gunter Thielen, Chairman and CEO of the Bertelsmann Foundation and Chairman of the Supervisory Board of the Bertelsmann Group, firmly rejected any attacks on the foundation's neutrality. According to Thielen, the foundation worked completely independently of the group's interests, a fact that was regularly verified by tax authorities and the foundation's supervisory board. Schuler, an experienced journalist who had had privileged access to Bertelsmann for some time, however, disagreed. Neither did the foundation's supervisory board check the foundation in the interest of the public nor did local tax authorities have the resources to audit thoroughly a multibillion euro company. Instead, the goal of the supervisory board was to keep away the public in the interest of the founder, the Bertelsmann Foundation, while tax authorities were notoriously understaffed (in Gerstenberg, 2008; also Schuler, 2010). Further, Schuler (2021) argued that, throughout recent history, Bertelsmann has been successful in suppressing critical coverage of the group, the foundation, and the Mohn family. This has rarely happened by means of direct intervention or censorship. Instead, the group owns major media outlets (i.e. press, television, radio) and can, thus, set the tone of its own coverage. It is also a major advertising source for other media outlets, and its high-ranking group managers maintain close relationships to owners, publishers, and editors of these, and other media outlets. Further, the foundation regularly floods the (German) information economy with its own reports and publications. All these influencing factors are part of the reason why Bertelsmann has been very successful in creating and fostering its narratives about its own institutions while also setting the tone for public debates and social issues at large.

What Schuler and others have shown (and what we had tried to show in this book) is that the power of Bertelsmann does not lie in the market alone. It lies in the push for synergies between all its market divisions and in its intertwined interests with the work of the Bertelsmann Foundation – one of the most influential and well-networked neoliberal think tanks in Germany with affiliated organizations worldwide. Although the Bertelsmann Foundation and the Bertelsmann Group are formally two separate entities, they are closely intertwined by means of shareholdings, central stakeholders, and interests. Put differently: "Bertelsmann won't do anything that's not good for Bertelsmann," no matter how much the foundation and/or group present their interests in the service of the public good. While the Bertelsmann Group is the largest media company in Europe, and can, thus, influence public opinion by means of its television, radio, and printing products, the Bertelsmann Foundation (by means of its networks, studies, and lobbying efforts) exerts long-term political influence on society at large. Meanwhile, different service divisions of the Bertelsmann Group provide hand-tailored solutions for issues put on the political agenda by the foundation. It is a circle of interlinking interests coming to full close. The number one rule, however, remains the same: Self-interests guide the way. In this sense, Bertelsmann is not different from other global players in the media and communication (service) market.

Unlike other multinational media and communication service providers, however, Bertelsmann has been in business for more than 180 years. It is a family business controlled by the Mohn family and the Bertelsmann Foundation. Reinhard Mohn, *the* key figure in developing the company into a major corporation and founder of the Bertelsmann Foundation, is an ever-present figure in both entities. On her 80th birthday, Reinhard Mohn's wife Liz Mohn passed the influential position of family spokesperson to her son Christoph Mohn, safeguarding the sixth-generation family control. This long history with its long-built experiences and infrastructures has been the consistent basis of continued growth for the company. Take for instance the book club model: in Communication and Media Studies, book club models are generally considered examples for a "democratization of reading," since they successfully brought the medium book to non-readers. From an economic perspective, however, the book club model is something completely different: it represents a kind of optimizing business strategy. In it, the greatest possible distribution of a small number of products is achieved by exploiting economy-of-scale advantages (Becker and Bickel, 1992, p. 135). Put differently, with its book club experience, the Bertelsmann Group became an experienced specialist in distribution concepts, distribution policies, and in the multiple exploitation of products, marketing, and shipping. It did not, however, simultaneously or necessarily become a dominant force in creativity, ideas, and new content (p. 136). This becomes especially clear when one looks at the group's subsidiaries, such as *Bertelsmann Investments* or *Arvato*, operating in completely different fields.

The group, with total revenues of more than 17 billion euros and nearly 130,000 employees worldwide (in the year 2020), is still one of the world's largest multinational media, information, and consulting groups. In fact, if the size of the group was calculated not according to annual sales but according to its creditworthiness with banks, the Bertelsmann Group, for many years, was the world's largest multinational information group. Unlike many U.S. corporations, it had operated debt-free (Becker, 2007, p. 3). With the acquisition of the world's largest general interest publisher *Random House* in 1998, the group became one of the most important media players also in the United States – though it had been buying massively into the U.S. media market since 1986. At the beginning of 2007, following the group's takeover of *Bookspan* from *Time Inc.*, Bertelsmann was even considered the country's largest direct provider of media (p. 4). By 2020, the United States accounted for 24.8 percent of the group's revenues, second after Germany (Bertelsmann Annual Report, 2020). This revenue share will certainly increase if the 2.2 billion US dollars bid to purchase the U.S. publishing company *Simon & Schuster* goes through. The deal would give *Penguin Random House* control of 70 percent of the literary fiction market in the United States and nearly one-third of all English-language book sales worldwide (Wood, 2021).

One key to Bertelsmann's success was the group's broad portfolio: From books to music and radio to magazines and the education business. There is no media product the group does not produce, and if anything, the Covid-19 crisis has shown that the loss of advertising revenues in one sector could be cushioned by other business areas. In 2020, the group had even higher profits of around 1.46 billion euros than the year before (1.1 billion euros). For some time now, however, Bertelsmann CEO Thomas Rabe and his top management have been focusing not only on a broad portfolio but also on interlinking synergies. This becomes particularly clear in the media market: the group is pushing (global) content exchange and joint ventures between different media divisions (e.g. more products created on a single topic, such as complementary podcasts or documentaries). Thus, while the current priority of the group is to build "national media champions" in its core markets, the group aims to also invest massively in its global content businesses. This comes in addition to expanding its global services businesses and to driving forward its online education activities around its anchor companies *Relias* and *Alliant* in the healthcare and technology sectors. A fifth priority involves expanding the number of digital holdings (Börsenblatt, 2021).

Whether or not these strategies work out in practice is of secondary importance. What matters most is that they show that thinking of Bertelsmann as a traditional media giant simply does not give credit to its corporate realities. The group has become a world leader in providing global media and communication *services* (e.g. global supply chains, financial flows, IT systems, and customer communications) and in online education (services). This is also due to its continuous investment efforts (e.g. in start-ups in media, services, and education, often with a focus on emerging technologies). While the Bertelsmann Group has always been innovative in its traditional book market efforts, it has also always been conservative when entering any new media and communication markets. Only after a phase of self-cleansing, when start-ups and young growth markets had proved themselves viable, would the group buy up existing and innovative smaller players or new technologies. Thereby, Bertelsmann would position itself at the top of any individual submarket with its concentrated power of a multinational corporation. Put differently, Bertelsmann "eats up" innovation. It does not operate at the grassroots level but it secures new markets from above.

With its growing focus on privatizing public services, it also becomes clear that Bertelsmann, in fact, *needs* the state. On the one hand, the state creates favorable legal frameworks for the activities of the Bertelsmann Foundation. Secondly, there is no better contractual partner for the service juggernaut *Arvato*. *Arvato* promises local governments, hospitals, or universities and schools that by providing economic indicators, it can "perform the miracle of combining a reduction in costs with an increase in quality everywhere at the same time" (Felder, 2000, p. 1095).[1] Bertelsmann, thus, has a strong interest in productively resolving central contradictions

---

1 Original: "überall zugleich das Wunder vollbringen zu können, eine Kostensenkung mit einer Qualitätssteigerung zu verbinden."

between its own corporate interest and its neoliberal pursuit (for instance, the contradiction between the negative definition of the role of the state and its continued importance for economical processes). With the growing privatization of public services worldwide and Bertelsmann's strong market role in providing these services, it can be expected that the group as well as the foundation will continue growing deeper into societies worldwide.

While this seems a bleak outlook, it cannot be stressed enough that this book has analyzed the corporate side of Bertelsmann. While this is a worthwhile endeavor, (almost) nothing has been said about the people working at Bertelsmann – that is, its 132,842 employees worldwide. This is a general blank spot in any analysis of global corporate structures. By describing corporate strategies, one runs the danger of unintentionally reproducing dominant power structures, giving the impression that these structures are unsurpassable. This, of course, is not the case. Whenever there are workers, there is resistance, there is cooperation and conflict. In Germany, there is also a growing opposition to the deep and broad involvement of the Bertelsmann Foundation in policy work, may it be on a local, national, or international level. The last words of this book are therefore dedicated to workers at Bertelsmann who have historically been fighting for better working conditions, and to the thousands of citizens in Germany and Europe who are becoming increasingly aware of (and active against) the deep-rooted political power of a corporation by means of its foundation.

References

Becker, J. (2007). Forschungspolitische Notizen zu meiner Bertelsmann-Forschung, unpublished. http://profjoergbecker.de/Dokumente/autobiotexte/2007%20Bertelsmannforschung.pdf [November 22, 2021].

Becker, J., and Bickel, S. (1992). *Datenbanken und Macht. Konfliktfelder und Handlungsräume.* Opladen: Westdeutscher Verlag.

Bertelsmann Annual Report. (2020). Retrieved from https://www.bertelsmann.de/media/investor-relations/einzelabschluesse/jahresabschluss-2020-bertelsmann-kgaa.pdf [February 5, 2022].

Börsenblatt. (2021, April 2021). Bertelsmann setzt neue strategische Prioritäten. *Börsenblatt.* Retrieved from https://www.boersenblatt.net/news/verlage-news/bertelsmann-setzt-neue-strategische-prioritaeten-175131 [January 5, 2022].

Felder, M. (2000). Verwaltungsmodernisierung, die Transformation von Staatlichkeit und die neue Sozialdemokratie. *UTOPIE kreativ,* (121/122), 1090–1102.

Gerstenberg, R. (2008, August 23). Nur im eigenen Interesse. *Deutschlandfunk*. Retrieved from https://www.deutschlandfunk.de/nur-im-eigenen-interesse-100.html [March 5, 2022].

Schuler, T. (2010). *Bertelsmannrepublik Deutschland: Eine Stiftung macht Politik*. Frankfurt am Main: Campus Verlag.

Schuler, T. (2021). Die andere Seite von Bertelsmann. *Wirtschaftsjournalist*, Vol. 3 (2021), 40.

Wood, H. (2021). *US Department of Justice sues to block Bertelsmann's S&S deal*. The Bookseller. Retrieved from https://www.thebookseller.com/news/us-justice-department-sues-block-bertelsmanns-ss-deal-1286740 [January 20, 2022].

Index

Alliant International University 17, 45, 62, 99
Amazon 2, 20–21, 25, 37, 43–44, 54, 64, 93–94
antitrust regulations 12, 41–43
Argentina 24, 39, 60–62, 65
Arvato 16–18, 33–38, 45, 52, 56–57, 60, 62–63, 65–66, 71–73, 81, 92, 98–99
Asia 19, 37, 50, 52, 56, 71, 93

Bantam Books 11, 40–41, 71
Barack, Obama 25–26
benchmarking 78–79
Bertelsmann-Stiftung (Bertelsmann Foundation) 1, 3, 75–82, 85–89, 96–97, 99–100
BMG 15–16, 29–32, 43, 45, 51–52, 55, 60, 62
book clubs 1, 12, 49, 51–54, 64, 92, 97–98
Brazil 2, 29, 39, 49, 60–62, 65, 72, 93

CAP 80–81
Center for Higher Education (CHE) 78–81
Chile 60–62
China 2, 4, 27, 29, 33, 39, 49–57, 71–72, 79, 91, 93–94
Christian company 6–7, 10, 92
Circulo de Lectores 63–64
Colombia 60–65
Content Alliance 16, 20

Dangdang 54–55, 60
diversity 21–22, 43

e-commerce 34, 36–37, 49, 51–52, 54–55, 57, 71
education 3, 15–17, 45–46, 62, 65, 71, 75, 77–78, 81–82, 93–94, 98–99
Elsevier 55
Europe 2–4, 11–12, 18, 20–22, 26–27, 29, 31, 34–36, 39–42, 50–51, 69, 71–78, 81–82, 85–86, 88–89, 93, 97, 100

Fremantle 16, 18–20, 45, 50, 52, 62

Google 2, 37
Groupe M6 18, 82
Gruner + Jahr (G+J) 15–16, 23, 26–27, 35, 50, 72, 91
Gütersloh 1, 6, 33–34, 77, 79, 86

Hong Kong 17, 52, 69, 71

India 2, 49, 72, 91, 93
innovation 34, 57, 80, 91, 93–94, 99
Ireland 66, 69, 71–73

Jewish History 7–9, 40

Latin America 4, 39, 45, 60–66, 94
Lesering 12–13, 34, 64, 92
lobbying 42, 78, 81–82, 85–88, 97
logistics 34–37, 41, 49, 52, 54, 57, 92
Luxembourg 18, 20, 69, 72

Majorel 34, 37–38, 45, 52, 60, 62
Mexico 17, 39, 60–66
Microsoft 2, 4, 17, 35–37, 42

Middelhoff, Thomas 1, 3, 7, 18, 42, 54
Mohn family 2–3, 6–7, 53–54, 75, 77–78, 89, 91, 94, 96–97
Mohn, Christoph 3, 6–7, 77, 97
Mohn, Elisabeth (Liz) 3, 6–7, 13, 77, 86, 92, 97
Mohn, Heinrich 7–9, 11
Mohn, Reinhard 2–3, 6, 8, 34, 40, 75–78, 91, 97

Nazi Era 6–11, 92
Netflix 20–21, 25, 31
Netherlands 18–19, 69, 71, 86

Penguin Random House 15–16, 24–26, 43–44, 46, 52, 55, 60–64, 66, 70, 98
Peru 60–61, 63, 66
profit-sharing 10, 91–92

Rabe, Thomas 17–20, 25–26, 98
racism 31, 42–43

revolving door 41, 85–86, 88
RTL 4, 15–22, 26–27, 41, 46, 50, 72, 91

Simon & Schuster 24–25, 43, 98
Spain 18, 24, 29, 34, 39, 60–61, 63–65, 72, 75
subsidiaries 2, 12, 29–30, 39, 45, 49, 52, 56, 60–62, 64–65, 70–72, 93–94, 98
synergies 16, 23, 27, 30, 97–98

tax havens 39, 69–73
transatlantic relations 39, 81, 87–89

United States 2, 4, 8, 12, 19–20, 24–27, 29–31, 34–35, 39–44, 45, 49, 54, 56, 61, 69, 71–72, 79, 85, 87–89, 93–94, 98
Uruguay 60–61, 63, 65

workers 42, 44, 57, 73, 92, 100

For Product Safety Concerns and Information please contact our EU representative GPSR@taylorandfrancis.com
Taylor & Francis Verlag GmbH, Kaufingerstraße 24, 80331 München, Germany

www.ingramcontent.com/pod-product-compliance
Lightning Source LLC
Chambersburg PA
CBHW051757230426
43670CB00012B/2321